THE BRADLEY EFFECT

JOHN MOREY ALLEN

ACKNOWLEDGEMENTS

It took many years to write this book, and it never would have been completed without several boots in the butt by my good friend, Charity Reed. Also, thanks to Ginny Vermillion, writer of several books, including *Dare to Dream*.

To my wife, Ryan, who married me for better or worse, but not for lunch.

Preface

So, you're traveling by air. You find yourself at LAX, Los Angeles Airport, at the International Terminal, whether this be your departure point or a stopover on your way to Puerto Vallarta or wherever. You grab your fast food or maybe a magazine, or if you're not on your way to Singapore, a pack of gum. Or perhaps Los Angeles could be your final destination.

Airports are fine places, insofar as they go, but they're really all just about the same. Nobody can truthfully say he likes being in airports. They are places where one is forced to spend periods of times between what he or she is really doing. Stressful and boring are what they are.

The International Terminal at LAX is one that is above average in its impressiveness. This one terminal houses twelve gates and nine satellite gates. Ten million passengers per year pass through this terminal, and this number will certainly increase as current expansion projects are completed.

The airport itself is the sixth busiest in the world. And this, the Tom Bradley International Terminal, bears the name of an outstanding former citizen. In fact, it was commemorated to him back in 1984. A gigantic bust of him stands at the entrance. Only a great man would be deserving of this tremendous honor. Yes, a former mayor, a leader of men, a pioneer in the struggle for blacks to finally achieve equality, someone of the twentieth century. Yes, a black man, a leader of blacks, residing in history between Martin Luther King Jr. and Barrack Obama. A man dedicated to humanity, a shining torch for all to follow, the most honorable, courageous, and wonderful man, a giant among men, the Honorable Thomas Bradley.

Hogwash!

1.

My new office was perfect. In a small town, wearing cowboy boots to work, knowing all the farmers and cowboys, I was, pardon the pun, in hog heaven. This was indeed a better situation for me than before I divorced in 1977 and worked in the Bay Area. Of course, the current law practice wasn't quite as lucrative as it had been when I had two full-time secretaries working for me. Now I even sometimes had to receive payment for my legal services by way of crates of apricots or almonds in lieu of cash. But that was OK. I like apricots and almonds, and I liked the people there. Country people, good, solid, leave-your-doors-unlocked kind of people. And honest people, by and large. Contrary to my legal training, which included the supposition that you really can't ever trust anyone, out here it seemed a handshake was just as good as a written, notarized document.

I have always had a thing about honesty. A little fib now and then is OK. If you really don't want to go to your brother-in-law's birthday party, then it's permissible to claim the flu; if your wife's new dress looks awful, you might not want to tell her that truth. But when it goes much beyond that, when it really means something, then it becomes a lie, and to me lying is just totally wrong. And to take advantage of someone through lies and deceit is just downright despicable.

After suffering the financial devastation that is common in a divorce (now more properly defined as dissolution of marriage), I was able to put a down payment on an old floating home situated atop the slow-flowing water surrounding Bethel Island on the California Delta. The Delta travels from San Francisco Bay eastward, where it branches somewhat northward into the Sacramento River, which travels to, you guessed it, Sacramento and eastward into the San Joaquin River, which extends to Stockton. There are many off-shoots from these rivers, which comprise one thousand miles of waterways, which wind around through fields that produce some of the best crops in the world. Corn, asparagus, and tomatoes are in abundance, to name a few.

The somewhat exotic name, Bethel Island, might conjure up a picture in one's mind of a luxurious place like, say, Balboa Island, inhabited by well-to-do people—a location with boutique shopping, restaurants, and other amenities. But such could not be further from this image. True, Bethel Island was, and is, an island. The only way on or off at the time was by way of a rickety, old bridge that could barely handle two cars traveling in opposite directions. The town had one main road, extending maybe a quarter mile, which contained most of the commercial businesses, including a grocery store with a Laundromat in the back, two real estate offices, and a couple of boat sales establishments. Throughout the entire island, there was a golf course, three or so trailer parks, and six bars. The inhabitants were friendly, down-home sorts, and many of these spent a lot of their time in the bars. Some had come here to escape from whatever they needed to escape from. If you ever read

Steinbeck's *Cannery Row*, then you understand the nature of the people and the atmosphere of Bethel Island in the late seventies.

To get to my floating home, you would go over the bridge onto the island, turn left, and travel about three-quarters of a mile. Then park off the edge of the road, cross an empty lot up onto the levee, and walk down the ramp from the levee to the door. Half of the structure was a dock area to accommodate my older twenty-eight-foot Trojan wooden boat. The remaining half of the home was enclosed. Therein was located an open area, which consisted of a combination living room and kitchen; and then there was the separate bedroom and bathroom. The entire structure rose and fell with the tides, and the fishing for catfish was good. To catch these fish, you didn't need any gear or bait; all you had to do was rope a tire to the dock and submerge it halfway into the water. The fish would swim into the tire and remain there until you'd pull the tire out and retrieve your dinner. Simple.

Along with fresh fish whenever you wanted it, nearby crops were available for the taking. Nothing is better than corn cut fresh from the field, boiled and slathered with butter. It's even better barbequed. Just don't make the mistake of taking cattle corn, which tastes just about as good as cardboard.

Ah, life was good there, out in the sticks with Max, my German shepherd. Plus, I had survived the marital split and even got to keep my guitar. Yes, life was good.

2.

There are two Brentwoods in California, the not-so-familiar city in the north and the famous city to the south, which is now referred to as the "OJ Brentwood" by many of the northerners. My new office was in the north and about three miles from my floating home. It was one of a suite of three offices in an old structure that abutted railroad tracks. Judging by the prolific weeds, a train had not utilized these tracks for many years.

The building itself was wood, single story, and had a porch all the way around. It sort of reminded me of the place where Judge Roy Bean must have sat in his rocking chair pronouncing men on horseback guilty of cattle thievery, and having them hanged right there in the yard.

The building was leased by another attorney, Don Piantanida, and his young secretary, Carole. Don had formerly worked as a deputy district attorney for Contra Costa County. There was also an insurance man, from State Farm, as I recall who occupied the second office. Don subleased the third office to me. Don and I agreed to share expenses, including Carole. The building may have been run-down, but Carole sure wasn't. She typed so fast, without errors, that the round metal ball on the IBM Selectric typewriter was constantly breaking.

The law practice itself was relatively low-key. We handled what came in the door. We took care of local real estate problems, minor personal injury cases, and contract matters. I was on the county's criminal referral panel and defended clients from all sorts of alleged wrongdoings, from DUIs to theft to battery matters. But in the area of criminal law, I restricted myself to representing clients who were charged with relatively minor crimes only.

Before moving my office to Brentwood in 1978, I had taken on the more serious cases. One such case was defending one of two men accused of raping a young woman who was visiting the Bay area. Through a series of events during the course of the case, which did not necessarily include my expert legal prowess, I was able to get him off the rape charge. He was released from custody. Naturally, I felt I was the very best criminal lawyer in the country. But two months later, I read in the paper that this same guy had been arrested for two more rapes. This was a major event for me. I felt so bad for the victim in that case, I knew I was not cut out to handle the defense of those accused of the most serious personal crimes. It was also a factor leading to my decision to move to the country to seek a more relaxed, easygoing life.

One evening a week, usually on a Friday, I would get together with Norm Halsey, a local artist, sign painter, and part-time cowboy, to have a few beers and play guitar. Sometimes other friends were there, sometimes not. We had terrific times, drinking beer, making up songs, drinking beer. We recorded our "sessions" on my cassette recorder. Later playback of the tapes revealed some fairly acceptable renditions, at least during the first hour or so. After that, it sounded pretty much like monkeys being attacked by other jungle animals. When things started getting out of hand, Max would get up off the floor and leave the room.

One of our songs, if I may say so, was really good. At the time Jerry Brown was governor of California, his first time around. Agriculture in the state was being severely rampaged by the Mediterranean fruit fly, one of the more destructive insects known to exist. Brown, the environmentalist, refused to permit aerial spraying, but rather suggested that the farmers strip their crops. Millions of dollars were lost, and this would have extended to billions of dollars if alternative action were not taken. It took President Ronald Reagan, himself a former governor of California, to solve the crisis by refusing to allow California's agricultural products to be exported from the state. The eventual solution was spraying the crops with malathion.

Our song was written from the viewpoint of the medfly himself. It was entitled, appropriately enough, "The Med fly Song." A portion follows:

Oh, I'm a Mediterranean fruit fly
They say I'll damage your fruit
They got my cousin
But I keep a buzzin'
Frankly I think I am cute

Governor Brown, well, he came into town
The farmers were down on their knees
He said, "This situation requires hesitation"
He told them to strip all their trees
Well, they set up a roadblock

15

For my family to stop
This would save their day
For my cousin it came hard, but I got my green card
And slipped right through OK

Well, Reagan examined, he said, "I've a plan" and
He ordered embargoes that day
He said, "Brown, you are cute, but there'll be no more
*   fruit from Cal-i-for-ni-ay."*
Well, Brown, he got mad and then he got glad
His eyes lit up like the day
The answer, of course, is to bring out the forces
With malathion spray.

We played this tape for our friends and everyone got a good chuckle from it. One who listened was our friend, Pat Kelley, who happened to be a disc jockey for KJOY radio station in Stockton. He liked it so much, he started playing it on the air in regular rotation. Well, this silly song took off. Other stations throughout the country copied the tape. I heard that it was being played as far away as Georgia, New Jersey, and even Alaska. It was also reported that the song was a favorite of long-distance truck drivers, who passed it back and forth on their CBs.

Not that it's important to the story here, nor is it even pertinent, but this song did eventually cost me $8,000 out of pocket because of my ill-fated attempt to make some money off it. We were advised that we needed to have an entire album, not just one song, if we were ever to be able to sell the product. So Norm and I took the boat and our guitars out on the river. We hastily wrote nine more songs and later recorded them at a home studio in Stockton. Norm did the artwork for the album cover, and our efforts were sent off for final production. Well, there were delays, such that when we finally received the final product, "The Med fly Song" had ceased playing on the radio stations. And so ended our music careers. Was it worth it? You bet it was!

3.

Although I certainly did not realize it at the time, March 10, 1981, was the day my life was about to take another unexpected turn. On that date I met John Bland and Ruth Barrett.

Our secretary, Carole, had scheduled an appointment for one John Bland, who needed a will. At the given hour, Mr. Bland appeared in my office. I led him through the door to a chair opposite my old and worn, oversized oak desk. A short, black gentleman in his eighties, very frail and infirm, Mr. Bland took off his coat and sat down. He was accompanied by a younger black woman, probably somewhere in her forties, heavyset, friendly and articulate, dominant. She introduced herself as Ruth Barrett, a friend of John's. Also in attendance was Ruth's husband, Nolan, who was smaller than herself and very soft-spoken.

The will that Bland wanted was simple. Ruth Barrett was to be executrix. His estate was to be divided equally between one Emerson Smith and a Francis Jeffries, both of whom resided in Los Angeles. Through our meeting I learned that Bland's "estate" was very small, negligible in fact. It hardly merited their being in a lawyer's office. But whatever. The will was prepared that afternoon and signed by him the next day. Carole and I witnessed his signature, I charged him $35, and that was that.

May and June are terrific months on the California Delta. Winter is gone. These are the months before the temperature gets up into the hundreds. The skies are beautiful, the water is calm. The delta waterways are shared by fishermen, house boaters, water-skiers, and partiers. Everyone is happy, unencumbered by the daily grind and the worries that accompany it. I spent many a day during those months in 1981 on the Delta in my boat. Sometimes I was with friends. Sometimes it was just Max and me.

Two months passed, and John Bland was back in the office with Ruth Barrett. They showed me a prior will that had been signed by Bland. In this will he had left everything to one Geraline Felder of Stockton, California. Felder had also been named executrix in that will. Bland related that Felder had taken care of him for a time during his illness. He related his shocked discovery that she had written checks from his checkbook to her own creditors and that she had stolen a ring valued at over $1,000. This ring had belonged to Bland's departed wife, Velma. Additionally, he alleged that he paid $2,157.39 to pay Felder's car off, and she refused to pay him back, despite her promises to do so. He wanted his money back.

Again, we were dealing with a situation that does not warrant the engagement of legal counsel. Nevertheless, I liked John Bland, and thus I wrote a letter to Felder. Felder had an attorney, Kingsford Jones of Menlo Park. He responded that he might have a conflict, because he had prepared the will for Bland. Before I could do anything, Bland called me off, stating that he did not want to pursue the matter further.

A year went by. Ruth Barrett came in to advise me that she had been caring for John Bland, and he wanted me to prepare a power of attorney so that Ruth could take care of his small financial dealings. I prepared the financial power of attorney, and it was signed by Bland on February 11, 1982.

Less than a month later, during the first week of March 1982, Ruth again was in the office to advise that John Bland had just died. She had been caring for him in her home until the time of his death. She showed me a new will, this one in Bland's own handwriting and dated February 22. In this holographic document, he had named Ruth as both executrix and sole heir of his small estate. I was not particularly anxious to spend much time on this matter due to the limited amount of assets involved and so advised Ruth. But then she told me something that really perked my interest.

Ruth told me that Bland had been constantly complaining to her that he had been involved in a transaction involving real estate that he had owned in Southern California and that he had been defrauded out of a substantial sum of money. He told her that the perpetrator of this fraud was Tom Bradley.

"Not *the* Tom Bradley?" I asked.

"Yes!" she replied. "*The* Tom Bradley, current mayor of Los Angeles and candidate for the governor of the State of California!"

Born in Texas in 1917, Thomas Bradley came to California when he was seven. He attended UCLA, where he was a track star. He was noted to be influential in breaking the racial barrier in college sports. In 1940 he joined the Los Angeles Police Department.

21

He attended and graduated Southwestern Law School in 1956. In 1961 he retired from the police department and started practicing law. He was elected to the Los Angeles City Council in 1963 and in 1969 he won the mayoral primary but lost the runoff with Sam Yorty. In 1973 he became the first African American mayor of a major city that did not have a black majority. In 1976 he was co-chair of the Democratic National Convention and was reelected mayor in 1977 and 1981. Then, in 1982, as the current mayor of Los Angeles, he was running for governor against the Republican nominee, George Deukmejian. And he was running hard. It was a hotly contested race, as most political races are, garnering daily news stories of everything that was happening.

Bradley was not a man to be taken lightly. He was, reportedly, a tall man, handsome, outwardly calm, but with an inner intensity. It was said that he was tough but his demeanor was smooth; he was friendly and gracious, but at all times, he was surrounded by armed bodyguards. He was extremely powerful and generally got what he wanted.

What if what Ruth told me was true? What if Bradley were a crook? Wow! I could see the headlines: "Mayor and Gubernatorial Candidate Perpetrated Fraud on Old, Infirm Guy." If he was what Ruth claimed, then the public should know about it. Many politicians are less than honest, but rarely does one rip off poor, old people. At least I had not heard of such a case.

4.

"Just what did Bradley do to John, Ruth?" I asked her.

"Well, I don't know exactly, but it has something to do with some real estate in Southern California."

"Are there any documents, or is there any paperwork relating to this?"

"Oh yes. John had boxes of paperwork. He'd been staying at my house up until he died. I can bring them if you want."

"Sure, bring them in."

Well, bring it in she did. Boxes upon boxes of paperwork. Papers and documents, old bills, tax papers, and possibly all pieces of paper John ever touched in his lifetime. Of course, nothing was in order. Just a haphazard random dumping of paper in boxes. I was sorry I had agreed to examine the "evidence." But curiosity was in control. I had to know if there was any truth to these allegations from the dead. Bradley, by all polls, was leading the race against Deukmejian for governor, and if it turned out that he did defraud

Bland, he had no business being dogcatcher of Lodi, much less the governor of the state.

I took all the boxes that Ruth Barrett had given me home in my pickup and laid them out on the floor. It took two days of sorting out the paperwork, throwing out all the old electric bills and the like, and then putting the relevant data in chronological order by date. Max was also curious, curious as to what I was doing; he wanted to help, but he just couldn't quite figure out how to do so. But he did understand, after I sternly instructed him that he was not to mess with the paperwork.

At about ten o'clock on the second night, the paperwork was in order chronologically. Over a glass of brandy, I examined the first document that could possibly be relevant. It was a grant deed dated February 6, 1945, from J. Monroe Nelson and Mary T. Nelson, husband and wife, transferring real property located in Riverside County to John Bland. Seeing that it was going to be a very long night if I continued with the project to reconstruct over thirty-five years of events, I called it a day.

The task resumed the following morning. The next document was a title insurance policy covering all three of them for $1,500. In 1949 Bland homesteaded the property, which consisted of approximately ten acres in the Moreno area, estimating its worth to be $5,000. The next document jumped ahead eight years, to 1957. It appears as though Bland borrowed $1,800 against the property from First Thrift of California. In August 1961 a deed of trust was executed, with the Bank of America being beneficiary. The trustor was John Bland, and now his wife, Velma, appeared as co-trustor. In November 1963 there was another loan wherein John and Velma Bland executed documents relating to their borrowing $9,500 from

Valley National Bank. It appears as though $6,500 of this sum went to the Bank of America to satisfy a debt Bland owed them.

John Bland had severe health problems that started in 1958 when he was injured on his job. A plywood wall form had fallen on him. The financial problems that ensued became unbearable. He underwent surgeries, which were unsuccessful in resolving his maladies. There was mention of possible medical malpractice in connection with the medical treatments. For years Bland was unable to work. His wife, Velma, also experienced health problems.

Tom Bradley's wife was Ethel. Ethel's father was cousin to John Bland's mother. It was natural for John to contact Tom Bradley, since Bradley was powerful, wealthy, and had many contacts. He was a lawyer. He knew lawyers. He had just been elected to the Los Angeles City Council, and he and John were related through their wives and thus were family.

On February 3, 1965, Bland sent a letter to Bradley in which Bland fully explained his legal and financial predicaments and asked Bradley for his advice and help as to what could be done to help Velma and himself. There is no documentation to show that Bradley ever responded to Bland's letter. It can only be presumed that he did not.

In March 1965 John and Velma contracted to sell the Moreno property in Riverside County for the sum of $45,000. They backed out of the deal, and Bland's broker, Iverson, sued them for his commission of $3,510 and secured a judgment.

On June 14, 1967, John and Velma had once again listed the property for sale using a new broker, this time for an asking price of $75,000. The property did not sell, and the original broker, Iverson, was to get the listing back in exchange for not proceeding upon his judgment. Although the facts here are unclear, it appears as though the property, in fact, was not listed.

Later in the year, it was evident to those who were aware that big things were about to happen in the Moreno area, including the property owned by the Blands. The State of California Department of Water Resources announced plans to construct a terminal reservoir near Perris as part of the Feather River Project. According to the design, the Blands' property would be affected. A portion of that property would be appraised and acquired by the Right of Way Department of the Division of Highways for the Department of Water Resources. The property was now prime real estate, although it does not appear the Blands were aware of this. There is correspondence evidencing that at least one real estate broker did contact the Blands in an attempt to list and/or purchase the property.

In November and December 1968, the Department of Water Resources wrote to the Blands, advising that construction of their facilities was moving ahead toward its 1972 completion date and that they would be acquiring a portion of Bland's property.

Documentation retrieved from the multitude of boxes supplied by Ruth Barrett indicated that there were perhaps other listings of Bland's property, but the details were not disclosed. It is known, however, that the property did not sell. It is also known that during this entire period of time, both John and Velma were in poor health and financially destitute. Other than this ten-acre piece of real estate, they had little, if any, assets.

5.

At the beginning of 1971, the Perris project was proceeding very nicely. It was now evident that this area would fully prosper. Land was at a premium.

Around this time, although the exact date is unknown, and just exactly how they got together is also unknown, Tom Bradley, his wife, Ethel, and John and Velma Bland did connect. On January 5, 1971, Bradley sent a handwritten letter to Bland on his personal stationery:

Dear John

I have started arrangements to borrow money for the sale of the property.
I suggest that you call at 6 p.m. on Thursday or Friday night for further discussion of the details.
Be prepared to let me know when you will be in Los Angeles.
Our phone is area code 213-294-xxxx.

Sincerely,
Tom Bradley

It is interesting to note here that Bradley says he was to borrow the money for the deal.

This is followed by another handwritten letter:

Dear John,

The papers have been prepared and are ready for signature. You can come in to Bank of Finance 2651 So Western Ave. 735-xxxx and see Mrs. Dean in the Escrow Department in the basement floor of the bank.
After you sign, you will have to have Velma sign by sending papers to her or taking papers to Palo Alto.
Call when you come to town. Home 294-xxxx or during day 485-xxxx.
Have secretary put your call through to me.

Tom

On January 17, 1971, a document with the heading "Agreement" was signed by John, Velma, and Tom and Ethel:

In consideration for the sale of ten acres of real property located at 28114 Brodisea Street, Moreno, California by John and Velma Bland, husband and wife, to Ethel and Thomas Bradley, husband and wife, for the sum of twenty-five thousand dollars, it is hereby agreed that upon the subsequent sale of the aforementioned property, the buyers Ethel and Thomas Bradley will share equally the net proceeds from the subsequent sale of the aforementioned property as follows: Upon sale, there shall first be subtracted from the proceeds of the sale all necessary costs of such sale, such as title search and policy, loan charges, escrow fees, etc. and all costs incurred by Ethel and Thomas Bradley in connection with the purchase of the property from Velma and John Bland and all subsequent payment of taxes, assessments, cost of maintenance, payments on the mortgage and other costs associated with the said property pending said subsequent sale. The net profit will then be computed by subtracting the aforementioned costs from the sale price of said property and the balance divided equally between the parties to this agreement.

So, effectively, the Bradleys were to purchase the property from the Blands for $25,000. When the property subsequently was to be sold by the Bradleys, they would equally divide the proceeds of that sale with the Blands after deducting all expenses incurred in both the sale to the Bradleys and sale by the Bradleys. Bradley would presumably provide an accounting to the Blands and distribute the proceeds accordingly. Unfortunately, the written agreement containing these provisions was not included in the escrow. There was no public record of the agreement. The records show only an outright sale of the property from the Blands to the Bradleys for $25,000. After payments to their creditors, the Blands received the total sum of $5,000.

At the point that Bradley was to sell the property, his total investment would be zero. Recall that in 1965, Bland could have sold the property for $45,000, but he had backed out of that deal. Now, in 1971, as shall be seen, the property was worth in excess of that sum, at least $55,000. In 1973 there was a negotiated sale for $100,000 (which did not consummate). The next year, in 1974, it actually sold for $110,000.

It is elementary to attorneys that they are ethically bound not to self-deal with clients. Bradley, a lawyer himself, should have referred Bland to another lawyer to review the contract for him, or at the very least, should have advised Bland that he had the right to do so. But he did not. Nor did he disclose the fact that he was a founder and principal in the company handling the escrow, the Bank of Finance.

Bland did not realize he had been taken until later, as we shall see. Any responsible lawyer would have advised Bland not to deal with Bradley but rather to sell the property on his own.

John Bland trusted Tom Bradley. He was family.

6.

The transaction with Bradley in no way assisted Bland in his and Velma's dire financial situation. They remained destitute. John applied for welfare. In a letter dated February 25, 1971, from the Department of Welfare of Riverside County, his application was not accepted.

Dear Mr. Bland:

Enclosed is the yellow form you recently returned to our office. We are unable to complete your reinvestigation without the completion of the starred (*) questions and your signature on the last page under #32.

We are most concerned over the ten (10) acres you own in Moreno. If this property has been sold we must be informed as to proceeds, terms of the sale, etc. If it has been sold please send a copy of the closing escrow statement. If it is for sale you must supply us with a copy of the listing as held by the realtor. If it is not being sold, or up for sale, you must come up with a plan to utilize this land in some way so that you can receive an income as welfare regulations stipulate. Please reply promptly.

Bland forwarded this letter to Tom Bradley, who on March 12, 1971, wrote the following letter to the Department of Welfare and sent it back to that department although he incorrectly identified that department as "Hall of Records":

Dear Mrs. Goehring:

Mr. John Bland asked me to send the enclosed information regarding the sale of 10 acres which he and his wife formerly owned in Moreno, California.

Mr. Bland had reached the point where he simply was unable to maintain payments on the property and made several efforts to sell it. In December of 1970 we began negotiating a sale. The liens on the property were so large in amounts that a reasonable sale price was not possible unless the amounts were reduced. Negotiations were then conducted with the lien holders and compromises were reached with several resulting in a reduction of almost $7,000. The sale was then consummated with the bank paying off all lien holders and mortgagors. Mr. and Mrs. Bland were paid $5,000 in cash to satisfy other creditors, but no cash was left to them.

If this information is not sufficient to answer all your questions, please feel free to contact me.

Very truly yours,

Thomas Bradley

"No cash was left to them." True. But what about the amount that would be coming to them when the Bradleys sold the property?

Should this have been reported to the welfare department? Does this constitute welfare fraud being aided and abetted by the mayor of Los Angeles and candidate for governor of the State of California? And why did he address the letter to "Hall of Records" rather than "Department of Welfare"? Why did he not clarify that the sale of the property was to himself? Deceptive at the very least, I would say.

Whoa! It was time for a break. On a crisp March evening, Max and I set off into the darkness of the country for a run, or more correctly, a brisk walk. Alternating between jogging and walking, I was trying to clear the myriad of thoughts clouding my mind. I might be representing Ruth Barrett, a black woman, friend of a poor, ill, weak, old, black man, now dead, who may have been conned by a highly influential man, extremely well regarded in the state—no, hell, in the country. A pillar of society, a leader of the black community. It was a damned good thing that my client was black, actually one of the few black people in the Brentwood area. Were it not so, would I be cast as a racist? Had Ruth been white, I might certainly be cast as such should I initiate an action against a prominent black man, especially during his contest against a white man, Deukmejian.

And what about the pressure if I were to embark upon such a project? I had come to Brentwood to get away from the big-city pressure. Did I really think I would be able to continue my relaxed lifestyle if I were to go up against Bradley? I was now a one-man, country lawyer with a shared secretary, and I surely would be up against a more-than-powerful law firm with unlimited resources. I would be legally outgunned at every turn. And what about the personal danger? Politics is a serious business to those who are involved. Bradley was an ex-cop, he had armed bodyguards.

On the other hand, if it were true that Bradley had defrauded this old man, John Bland, and possibly the State of California itself, then he certainly should not be governor. And, from all the polls, which decisively showed that he was far ahead and would be the winner, he would head the state for at least four years, maybe eight.

I didn't sleep well that night.

7.

By 1971 and before, Bradley was fully aware of the value of this ten-acre parcel of real estate. In May, he and Ethel deeded 0.712 acres of the property to the government for a major road that was going in abutting the property, which would connect Highway 60 with the new Lake Perris. Lake Perris was to be the last source of water supply for the Los Angeles area. It was also to be a major recreation area. Those in the know would prosper immensely. Bradley was in the know.

Bradley wrote a letter to Bland providing a partial update as to progress in the area. The copy of this letter is somewhat illegible, but it does contain the statement, "The road past our place will probably start in January and will be finished by August." *Our place?* Somewhat misleading? A lie? Yes. In fact, it was not "our" place. It was Bradley's place, and if John were to die, Bradley could keep all the money received from a sale, because there would be no record of any monies owed to John or Velma nor any record of their interest.

During 1972 and 1973, the major newspapers carried the story of the progress and eventual dedication of the massive construction project. All the while, Bradley was kept up to date on developments in the area by the project manager of the Southern California Financial Corporation.

In June 1973 the Bradleys contracted to sell the property for $100,000. Terms were $29,000 down, with a balance of $71,000, 8 percent interest, to be secured by a note and deed of trust. Broker's commission: $10,000. The buyer backed out, and the deal was not consummated.

On July 11, 1974, the Bradleys contracted to sell the property to Bradley Ltd., a limited partnership for the sum of $110,000. This sale materialized. The deed of trust shows the partnership address to be 28114 Brodiaea Avenue, Moreno, California. This is the former address of the property itself. The deed of trust is typed rather than signed: "Bradley Ltd., a limited partnership, By: TRV Inc., a corporation, General Partner." Below that are the signatures of Thomas R. Villelli and Richard A. Villelli. According to the notarization, Thomas was president of TRV Inc., and Richard was assistant secretary.

Bradley Ltd.'s agreement of limited partnership shows an identical date as the contract itself, July 11, 1974. General partner is TRV Inc., with 20 percent interest and eight named limited partners at 10 percent each.

It seems as though the actual sale occurred prior to the contract for the sale itself. The records show a note for $81,000 payable to Thomas and Ethel Bradley and a deed of trust, both dated June 21, 1974, both signed on behalf of Bradley Ltd. The closing papers were not in the cardboard boxes supplied to me by Ruth Barrett. But subsequent tax returns show that the Bradleys received $29,000 in cash, and from that paid the $10,000 commission and paid off to the bank the money used to do the deal with the Blands.

At this point Bradley had received $29,000 in cash, which he used to repay his loan, the interest thereon, and the broker's commission, and he had a one-half interest in the $81,000 note. Bland previously had received the benefit of having about $23,000 of his debts paid off, received $5,000 in cash, and presumably had a one-half interest in the $81,000 note.

So, what's wrong with this picture, one might ask. They're just about even. It was a fair transaction. Wrong. First of all, Bland could have sold the property himself in 1971 for $55,000. After commission, costs, and his debts were paid, he would have netted cash of over $25,000. Had he been able to wait until 1974, when the property sold for $110,000, he would have netted over $80,000.

Bradley would later contend that he pulled Bland up from behind the eight ball—that Bland had nowhere else to go, that he saved him. This is a fair argument except that had Bland known the value of the land and what was going on with the vast development project, he could have sold the property himself at any point.

Perhaps the most glaring wrongdoing here, at least in my eyes, was that there was no record of the Blands having any residual interest in this deal whatsoever. There was no mention of any dealings with Bland in the escrow or anywhere else. Should this frail, ill, couple in their eighties die, as was reasonably certain to occur, who's to say that Bradley could not bury the whole transaction with the Blands and keep the money? Now, I'm not saying this is definitely what would have occurred; what I am saying is that it was a possibility. And, as the reader shall soon discover, my dark, suspicious thoughts were to materialize into fact.

As I have previously mentioned, self-dealings by attorneys with uninformed clients and non-attorneys are unethical and are to be avoided at all costs. They can be cause for disbarment. Had Bland had his own attorney, his written agreement with Bradley, if there were to be one at all, would have been entirely different.

8.

On July 23, 1974, Bradley wrote the Blands to advise them that escrow had closed and purportedly provided an accounting. To be noted is the fact that Bradley deducted all principal and interest payments made on his loan to buy the property from the Blands, as well as any and all expenses incurred for everything ever connected with the property.

Dear John and Velma,

At last, the escrow has closed on the sale of the property in Riverside.
The following is a summary of the agreement and the figures in the entire transaction.
In March 1971 the sale and transfer from you to me and Ethel occurred with the agreement that we would borrow $25,000 to pay off your obligations. Escrow agreement is enclosed.
Ethel and I agreed that, upon sale of the property, we would share equally in the net proceeds from the sale. The net would be determined by subtracting all expenses incurred by Tom and Ethel in payment on the loan of $25,000, taxes and other costs pending or during the sale of the property.

Those costs are as follows: Payment to the Bank of Finance
on the loan. At rate of $175 per month. The total inter-
est was $5,111.22 and principal of $1,713.78—total of
$6,825. Taxes—1971—$733, 1972—$613, 1973—$543,
1974—[illegible].

There undoubtedly were more pages of this letter, but they were
not to be found.

On April 5, 1975, Bradley forwarded federal and state tax returns
for 1974 to the Blands that he had prepared for them. The returns
state that taxes on the property transaction were attributable 50
percent to the Bradleys and 50 percent to the Blands. Bradley attributed one half of the gross sale price, or $55,000, to the Blands
and attributed a long-term gain of $13,078 to them for the year,
as well as interest income of $2,574. Bradley paid the taxes due to
the IRS of $906 and Franchise Tax Board of $67 on behalf of the
Blands, which made it even more circumspect. A portion of the
letter itself follows:

Dear John and Velma

The US and California tax forms have been prepared by the
firm of Jules Glazer in Beverly Hills. We owed taxes on the
sale of the property in Moreno. As you can see, the $110,000
sale price is divided in half and the gross sales price for you
is $55,000, just as it is for me. The expense of the sale is
$10,000 brokers fee for the sale plus the escrow costs. That
divides into $5,395 for you and a similar amount for us.
The total we realized in 1974 was divided and it amounts to
$14,500 for each.

On June 5, 1975, Bradley sent the Blands a handwritten letter with a check for $415.50, claiming that this sum represented the sum due them under their agreement.

Dear John and Velma,

Enclosed is a check for $415.50, which represents your share of the payment on the Moreno property. This figure is the amount we agreed upon in accordance with the Letter of July 23, 1974. [In fact, there was no such agreement].
This reflects a half share of $491.50 less the $76 reimbursement to Ethel and me for money paid on the property but not covered by the cash left after costs and brokers commission was paid.
The buyer advanced interest from Jan to May, in order to provide enough money to close escrow. There was no cash left from the sale. In fact, I had to pay $149 to pay the deficit in order to close escrow.
I must remind you that these payments are taxable and you should ____your total income. ____enough to pay taxes, they will be due April 15, 1976. ___be glad to assist you in prepar your returns.
If there are any questions call me.

Sincerely,

Tom Bradley

9.

The years passed. Things were not going at all well for John Bland. According to his letter of February 28, 1979, to Ethel's older sister, Maggie, he was devastated that Tom and Ethel Bradley would not help him out in his time of need. John desperately needed a bank loan for $5,000, but could secure one only if Tom or Ethel would cosign for him at the Bank of Finance, of which Bradley was a founder and co-owner. However, they refused to do so. Bland felt he had been mistreated by them, and he simply could not understand why. The letter was long; a few pertinent excerpts follow:

Dear Maggie:

Maggie, I want you to know that I have not been talk to Marrie or Frandig about Ethel or our business. The reason I hung up on Ethel was because she haven't been right by me. She know that I should have been receiving some interest in our business transaction. I left the business for Ethel to take care of because I was sick during that and I could handle it myself. But it seems that no one had my interest at heart. I could have sold the place for $55,000 cash paid half of it on for me and took care of my business with the other half. But I'm living off of social security and the little money they send me and living in an apartment costing me $300 a month. Time are hard as you must know and anytime your family will allow you to be down and out like I am now then that cause enough to be up set. That's why I called Ethel and ask them to co sign for $5,000 for me. Because that how much it would take for me to move into an apartment. I found out from the bank that the $5,000 would be no problem to get if Tom would have co sign for me. He and Ethel owe me over $2,900 and it seem that they could co sign for me without even giving it a second thought. Maggie I don't understand why they would do me this if they loved me.

I found out that the boat landing on the property was Tom's son he's making money out of that and I can't even get interest off the __he owes me. That no kind of business. The whole thing seems like Watergate to me and I'm getting the bad end of it all. You said that they're not hard up for the money well then why do I have such a hard time getting mine $5,000—shouldn't have been nothing to ask for. So they're not hard up. You ask me not to let them down but it's not me who's letting you see it's them that are letting me down. I don't believe in gossiping and I don't want to make my business everybodies business anyway. But I feel that Ethel has used me for her own gain. As far as the love goes. I love all of you the family. We're cousin but family and I do love all of you. God has brought me to these 80 year and I've never done anybody any wrong and I don't plan to start now.

As I read this letter, I realized that I was building a rather intense dislike for the Bradleys and that it was likely I would be meeting them sometime in the near future.

Bradley got wind of Bland's discontent, because Bradley sent him a letter, dated March 13, 1979, to express his shock and surprise. He was indignant. In the letter he states that John is his "partner." He does not acknowledge any ownership interest in the boat landing referred to in Bland's letter, and at this writing, I do not know if any side deals were made or not.

To give Bradley the full benefit of the doubt, I have never alleged that any side deals took place, nor do I claim that Bradley had any interest in Bradley Ltd., although at the time I certainly had suspicions.

In any event, the records attached to Bradley's letter show that payments on the $81,000 note in the sum of $983 per month commenced on June 3, 1975, and continued to the date of his letter. From Bland's share, Bradley had been deducting $76 per month over the years for "expenses." After this letter was written, Bradley ceased taking this sum each month.

To add to the misery of the John Bland tale, his beloved wife, Velma, died.

10.

OK, so that was it! I had weeded out the reams of extraneous and irrelevant documents contained in the boxes; I had put the ones that remained in chronological order by date. Now I went through them and extracted other papers I had originally thought might be relevant but were not. Another two readings, and I had the basic idea of what had transpired from 1945 to 1982, some thirty-seven years.

Just what did I have? I asked Max and he was absolutely no help. All he did was scratch the door to go outside to do his business. An omen? Would this really be a pissy case if I were to continue?

Well now, let's see.

It's March of 1982. We have the mayor of LA running for governor in a hotly contested race. He is leading, according to the polls. He's a black guy running against a white guy. My client, Ruth— if I take the case—is black. John Bland was black. If I proceed, what, if any, effect would this have on the outcome of the election? Bradley is all-powerful. My people are powerless. How much does race play into all of this? What will I be up against if I proceed? Undoubtedly, some very fine lawyers with unlimited resources. Who's going to pay for all this? If it should become necessary to file a lawsuit, where would it be filed? In Los Angeles? Hell, I can't afford to be running back and forth to LA. Was his wife, Ethel, involved in all this? She did knowingly sign the paperwork, and she did receive the same benefits as her husband. What about the press? Surely they would be interested. They love bad news and controversy. But maybe not. By and large, they're a pretty liberal bunch and probably favor Bradley to win. If I proceed, would I be in physical danger? Probably not, but you just never know. Would we win? If so, what would or could we win? What if we lose? It would be a tremendous undertaking, both from financial and time expenditure standpoints.

I let Max back into the house. He totally ignored me, plopped down on the carpet, and promptly fell asleep.

All my senses were telling me not to mess with this matter. Things happen. And bad things often happen to good people like John and Velma. Life often is not just. And all wrongs cannot be righted. But good people should win! Karma should win out every time. Shit! What a decision!

What kept coming into my brain was this: If Bradley really did what it appeared he had done as contained in the paperwork in front of me, then he had acted dishonestly and unethically. And a dishonest, unethical person should not be put in charge of the State of California!

I also realized that my duty as an attorney was only to my client, who would be Ruth Barrett, executrix of the estate of John Bland. My duty as an attorney was not to the State of California or its people or to George Deukmejian or anyone else. Only to Barrett and indirectly to John Bland.

I decided the only way to go was to test the waters. I would write to Bradley and see what would happen. I fully explained my thinking to Ruth, and we executed a retainer agreement. On March 12, 1982, I sent a letter to Mr. and Mrs. Bradley.

Dear Mr. and Mrs. Bradley:

I represent Mrs. Ruth Barrett, named Executrix in the Will of John Bland. I regret to advise you that Mr. Bland died last week. At the present time, we are in the process of determining the nature and amount of assets and liabilities of Mr. Bland.
I would very much appreciate your advising me as to the nature and remaining amount owing to Mr. Bland in order that we may be apprised of all information pertaining to his estate. Thank you very much for your cooperation in this regard.

Very truly yours,

John Morey Allen

I did not receive a response to my letter, so on April 9, 1982, I followed up:

Dear Mr. and Mrs. Bradley:

Unfortunately, you have not responded to my letter to you dated March 12, 1982.
Additionally, I am advised that you have stopped payment on a check which is payable under your obligation to Mr. Bland. May I once again reiterate the necessity of your providing me with information concerning this obligation. I am about to

49

open an estate for my client as Executrix of the Estate of Mr. Bland, and I am sure that you will understand the necessity of providing this information.

Should I not hear from you within ten days, there will be no alternative but to proceed accordingly.

Thank you for your cooperation.

Very truly yours,

John Morey Allen

11.

I received a letter dated April 22, 1982, from Tom Bradley. Contained with the letter were two enclosures. The first was the copy of Bradley's letter of March 12, 1971, to the welfare department; the second was the copy of the escrow document dated February 11, 1971, showing the sale of the property to him for $25,000.

Dear Mr. Allen:

In reply to your recent inquiries re Mr. John Bland, please be advised of the following.

Mr. Bland, who was a cousin of my wife, owned property in Moreno, California. He owed debts on the property and other matters of about $25,000. He was unable to sell the property and was about to lose it. He came to my wife and me and indicated that he would rather give us the property if we would pay the obligations instead of losing everything.

We agreed to pay the debt and pay the Blands $5,000. That was done as you will note from the escrow record. The title was transferred to me and my wife on Feb. 11, 1971.

Although, by the terms of our agreement, there was no further obligation to Mr. Bland following the sale of the land

in 1974, I have sent him half of the monthly payments I
received.

When I learned of his death the day the last check was to be
delivered to him, I stopped payment.

I am enclosing some documents which relate to this matter.

I'm sorry for the delay, but have been too busy to write.

Very truly yours,

Thomas Bradley

This letter confirmed my suspicions that yes, this guy, Bradley,
was a man who was less than honest and less than ethical. It was
now abundantly clear that Bradley had intentionally deceived John
Bland and taken his money. The letter clearly states, "although,
by terms of the agreement, there was no further obligation to Mr.
Bland, following the sale of the land in 1974…"

The attached copy of Bradley's letter to the welfare department
(which he had addressed to the Hall of Records) proved to me, by
a preponderance of the evidence, that it was designed to deceive
that department so that Bland could get welfare, and was, along
with the attached escrow document sent to me, to deceive me into
believing there was nothing owing to Bland.

My suspicions were confirmed by Bradley's own pen. From the very
beginning of his dealings with John Bland, he had orchestrated the
plan that there would be no evidence of Bland's entitlement to the
remaining one-half interest in the $81,000 note once John was
dead. He knew that the obligation under the note would survive
Bland's life. And he would have gotten away with it had Bland not
thrown all of his paperwork into those cardboard boxes.

One thing did perplex me. Why on earth would Bradley go through all these deceptions when there was not a great amount of money involved? True, it was a lot of money to John Bland, but to a man like Bradley, a lawyer, the mayor, it was a very small amount indeed. Perhaps he simply could not control himself. Maybe it was built into his DNA. As I was to discover, this was not the first time that the direction of Bradley's moral compass came into question.

At least one sentence in his letter was entirely true. He was busy. The gubernatorial race was heating up. News concerning the upcoming election was constantly in the papers and on television.

12.

On April 27, 1982, I sent the following letter to Mr. Bradley:

Dear Mr. and Mrs. Bradley:

Thank you for your response dated April 22, 1982. I can well understand that you are busy at the present time due to your well-publicized endeavors; I am, at this time, in need of additional information from you in order that the Estate of John Bland may be fully apprised of all events which have transpired in your real estate dealings with Mr. Bland.
As I understand the situation, you and your wife purchased the Moreno property from Mr. Bland in 1971 for $25,000. It is further my understanding that you sold the property to Bradley Ltd. in June of 1974 and carried back a note of $81,000. I am advised that you had an agreement with Mr. Bland to borrow money to pay off his debts, then to sell the property, and then to split the sale price. There apparently was a signed agreement, wherein Mr. Bland agreed to subtract the sum of $76 per month from the $983 payment due under the Note in order to repay expenses incurred in the transaction. Reportedly, Mr. Bland had made various accusations against yourself and you thereafter agreed not to subtract the $76 per

month in the future and advised Mr. Bland that he would receive the sum of $491.50 thereafter.

From the facts which I presently have at hand, it would appear as though Mr. Bland's estate is entitled to one-half of the
remaining balance due under the Promissory Note.

I would very much appreciate your providing me with further
information concerning this matter.

Thank you for your cooperation. I look forward to hearing
from you.

Very truly yours,

John Morey Allen

I received Bradley's reply dated May 8, 1982:

Dear Mr. Allen:

I have searched for the copies of correspondence and other
documents relating to John Bland and the Moreno property.
Thus far I have not been able to find the material. I will continue to look among the large collection of materials dispersed
in three locations.

It will be appreciated if you will send me a copy of any documents you or Mrs. Barrett may have.

Also, please send me a copy of Mr. Bland's will. Can you tell
me what connection Mrs. Barrett has to this matter inasmuch
as I do not know her, nor do I recall her name having been
mentioned at any time by Mr. Bland.

Looking forward to hearing from you soon.

Very truly yours

Tom Bradley

I read this letter over and over again. I can tell you that I was nervous, very nervous indeed. My law associate, Don Piantanida, and secretary, Carole, were even more nervous than I.

Bradley's claim that he could not find his documents seemed doubtful. Clearly, what he was saying is, "What do you have?" In other words, "Do you have any proof of any outstanding obligation to Bland? If you do, you are the only one in the world who has proof of the fact that I engaged in unethical dealings."

It was clear that Bradley knew we had something on him, something he would not like to have exposed for all to see. He knew he had lied to Bland, he planned to cheat his estate out of money that was to be coming under the note, he had deceived the Welfare Department of the State of California, and now he was attempting to deceive me. I was confident he would not want this news to get out to the press or to the campaign of his political opponent.

So yes, I was nervous.

That night a strange thing happened. My floating home was located on that slough behind the lot at the edge of the dirt road. It was dark. Hardly anyone ever came there during the daytime, much less at night. At night no one ever ventured down that road unless invited.

It was just short of eleven o'clock when I saw headlights approaching. As the vehicle came within one hundred yards of my home, it stopped, and the lights were turned off. Five minutes elapsed. At this point I let Max out of the house. Nothing could be more intimidating than this animal unless he knew you. After five minutes went by, the car backed out down the road and was gone. But the lights never came back on. Maybe it was nothing. But the event certainly did nothing to calm my nerves.

13.

It is amazing what nervousness, when it accelerates to a level of apprehension, can do to a person.

Imagined or real, I did believe there was the distinct possibility that I could be in danger of personal harm. I possessed damning information against an already powerful person with even more lofty ambitions. If the voting public were to become aware of this information, it could certainly strike a serious blow to these ambitions, perhaps even destroy them. It seemed to me that it was possible that Bradley would not be about to allow some country lawyer to stand in the way of his attaining the exalted position of governor of California.

14.

The series of events described thus far in the Bland matter do not represent the first time Tom Bradley was accused of cheating family members.

On December 21, 1970, a civil lawsuit, Los Angeles Superior Court Case No. C992651, was filed as *Howard Lee Bradley, Thomas Bradley et al., Plaintiffs v. Thomas Bradley, Metropolitan Insurance Company, et al., Defendants.* The complaint petitioned the court to "Impress Constructural Trust and Order Reconveyance."

It was alleged that the defendant was Thomas Bradley, Los Angeles City Councilman, Tenth District, and the plaintiffs were Howard Lee and Thomas, the surviving sons of Howard Bradley, the councilman's deceased brother.

Howard Bradley had died on October 30, 1970, leaving his sons, Howard Lee and Thomas, as his only heirs. In his will Howard Bradley appointed his brother, defendant and attorney Councilman Tom Bradley, as executor of his estate and as trustee for his sons' inheritance. The will specifically mentioned real property in Los Angeles and a $21,000 life insurance policy, which were entrusted to defendant Bradley for equal distribution to the sons as he, defendant Bradley, deemed appropriate.

Documents recorded at the Los Angeles County Recorder's Office reveal that on September 21, 1970, defendant Bradley conveyed the decedent Howard's power of attorney to the trustee, himself. On the same date, he altered the title of the real property from sole tenancy of Howard to one of joint tenancy, naming Howard and himself as co-owners. Subsequently, a "Death of Joint Tenant Deed" was filed transferring sole ownership of the property to defendant Thomas Bradley.

In addition, the court file shows that defendant Bradley was designated as beneficiary of the $21,000 life insurance policy.

The complaint alleged that defendant Bradley failed to perform as trustee to his brother's estate in that he claimed unconditional title to the entire estate. It was further alleged that he had fraudulently defrauded Howard's sons out of their rightful legacy. Defendant Bradley defended by supplying the plaintiffs with an itemized list of loans he claimed to have made to his brother over a period of years. The sum of these loans was approximately $3,500.

The codefendant in the case, Metropolitan Life Insurance Company, deposited the $21,000 with the court clerk and requested that the court declare them not a party to the action. This request was subsequently granted.

A jury trial was scheduled for May 10, 1973. Prior to that date, on April 19, a settlement conference was held. A settlement was reached on that date. The case was settled; the records were ordered sealed.

In 1969 Tom Bradley had been on the Los Angeles City Council for six years. In that year he ran for mayor. He won the mayoral primary, but lost the runoff to Sam Yorty. Now, in 1973, he was again running for mayor against Yorty. Again, it was a bitter battle between the two.

On April 19, 1973, the date the lawsuit against Bradley was settled and the record sealed, the *Los Angeles Times* ran a front-page story captioned "Bradley Attempted to Steal Brother's Estate, Yorty Says." At a Rotary Club meeting, Yorty stated that Bradley attempted to steal his dead brother's estate from the brother's two sons and proceeded to detail the events of the lawsuit. He stated that the matter had not been publicized previously because of the press's obvious favoritism of Bradley.

"This is the type of outrageous and irresponsible statement that has been typical of the tactics of Sam Yorty for 40 years in public office," Bradley said. "It is the big lie technique."

Yorty said the matter was set for trial May 10, and "it would be very embarrassing for him [Bradley] to have to testify in a trial where he is trying to cheat those kids out of their estate and I predicted it would be settled once they knew we knew about it because somebody asked about it at a press conference, although you never heard about it. So, this morning, it was settled to the satisfaction of all the parties. So those two kids owe a great debt of gratitude to this campaign because he didn't dare continue to try to steal his dead brother's estate from the two kids."

Bradley replied that Yorty was wrong when he said he, Bradley, had his brother put anything in the will. "The person making the will indicates how he wants the will made out. That's what happened."

He went on to tell the press that he wished that Yorty would stick to the issues and not resort to employing these "tactics of outrageous lies."

Yorty also discussed the issue of racism in the election when he told the Rotarians that Bradley would benefit from a black bloc vote. "Now some people say that's racism," he said. "It's not racism on my part. It's racism on their part. He starts with a great big bunch of votes based on racism because they really don't know him. Blacks vote for Bradley because he is black. The lighter the vote is in the other sections of the city, the bigger that bloc becomes. So we have a problem if we are going to save our city and not have the kind of leadership reflected in the lawsuit settled this morning."

Bradley went on to win the election and in doing so, became the first African American mayor of a major city without a black majority. Reportedly, he had won every ethnic and geographical vote in the city.

One reporter who worked for Bradley on the campaign and who later became his press secretary, observed that immediately following the election, Bradley constantly received death threats. When he traveled by car, he had a rifle placed at his feet, and an LAPD helicopter shadowed his every movement. And of course, his ever-present bodyguards stayed near.

Bradley was reelected as mayor in 1977 and again in 1981.

15.

When John Bland died on March 5, 1982, he did not leave a large estate, to say the least. He was receiving the sum of $469.71 per month as his percentage of an old personal injury case; these payments were scheduled to terminate in 1984. He also had $3,500 in a bank account. The only other known asset subsequently discovered was his one-half interest in the note that Thomas Bradley did not acknowledge. There was a $600 creditor's claim from the funeral home that had to be paid.

On April 18, 1982, I filed documents on behalf of Ruth Barrett with the Contra Costa Superior Court Probate Department to have her named as executrix of Bland's estate and as heir under his holographic will dated February 22, 1982. Notice was mailed to those of Bland's relatives believed to be still alive. On December 22, 1981, exactly two months before his holographic will, Bland had a will prepared by an attorney in which he, Bland, bequeathed his estate in equal shares to his sister, Louise Smith, and his brother, James Bland, both from the Los Angeles area.

I really did not anticipate any problems regarding the administration of the estate of John Bland. The value of the estate was approximately $15,000. I had not included the Bradley note in the estate because I had no recorded documents to prove Bland's interest in the note, and I had yet to hear back from Tom Bradley, despite him saying he would check his records and get back to me.

On June 15, 1982, lo and behold, I was served with a "Contest and Grounds of Opposition to Probate of Purported Will." This document was filed by an attorney from Oakland by the name of Felix Stuckey. It was filed on behalf of John Bland's sister, Louise Smith. The paperwork alleged first that the holographic will was not entirely written, dated, and signed in the handwriting of the decedent and that it was a forged document. Second, it was alleged that the document was made as a result of undue influence by Ruth Barrett and was not Bland's will. It went on to say that Ruth had controlled Bland and had used undue influence upon him.

Attorney Stuckey did not contact me prior to his filing his pleading. Usually attorneys will discuss their disputes prior to the filing of accusatory pleadings, but no such discussions occurred in this case. This is particularly true when the amount at issue is so small. It is often more prudent to settle financial issues among the parties than to enter into a full-blown legal battle in the courts. Is it possible that there was some other reason Attorney Stuckey had filed these papers to contest Barrett's entitlement to Bland's estate? Certainly there was! If Ruth Barrett could be erased from the picture as not being a rightful heir, then who would there be to assert Bland's rights under the Bradley note? Nobody! Nobody besides Ruth, myself, and those close to us were privy to the details surrounding Bland's agreement. And it was exceedingly doubtful that Bland's sister, Louise, or her attorney, Felix Stuckey, knew anything about the Bradley-Bland real estate dealings.

One possibility that certainly existed—in my view, a probability—was that Stuckey was filing this will contest with the court at the direction of either Tom Bradley or someone working for him. The filing of this contest would certainly delay the determination as to whether Ruth was Bland's rightful heir and thus whether she was entitled to proceed against Bradley under the obligation under their agreement. As probate matters generally proceed quite slowly within the court system, the delay would cause the matter not to be decided until well after the November gubernatorial election.

And so, on June 17, 1982, I contacted Mr. Stuckey, the attorney, who happened to be African American. He advised that, yes, he was seeking a jury trial but that his financial arrangements with his client, Louise Smith, had not been worked out. Since I was still apprehensive about the possibility of physical danger to myself, I told Stuckey that complete copies of my files and all documents were in the hands of no fewer than three other attorneys.

The next day I received a telephone call from the Associated Press inquiring as to what was going on. The reporter read me his proposed news story and told me Bradley had been contacted and had stated he was waiting to see who was entitled to the money before he paid. The reporter told me his editor had the article and it would not appear until Monday, June 21.

On June 18, 1982, I filed an answer to the contest, in which I claimed that Louise Smith and Bland's other brothers and sisters had acted in concert with Thomas and Ethel Bradley to breach the contract between Bland and the Bradleys. I further alleged that all of Bland's brothers and sisters and the Bradleys had exerted undue influence over Bland.

On June 21 I called the reporter, who advised me that his editor had killed the story.

At this point in time, I was pissed. It was obvious to me that Tom Bradley was only months away from being elected governor and this just simply could not occur, in my view. With the concurrence of my client, Ruth Barrett, I contacted the Committee to Elect George Deukmejian to see if I could be of help. I advised the person who answered the phone that I was an attorney and that I was engaged in a dispute with Tom Bradley, their opponent. My call was greeted with a great deal of skepticism, naturally so. They had no idea if I was some sort of crank or what my true motives in making the call might be.

I received a return call from a man who identified himself as Rod Blonien. He was a special assistant attorney general for the California Department of Justice. He was also heavily involved in the Deukmejian campaign. Decidedly cautious, he asked me many, many questions: who I was, the nature of the dispute, my motives for contacting the campaign, what documentation I possessed. Apparently becoming convinced that I was not a total whack job or working for the Bradley campaign, he became interested in hearing more. I advised him that I had the consent of my client, and consistent with not breaching any ethical duties owed to her and without causing any prejudice to her legal case, I would be willing to disclose to him documents that we possessed in that case.

A rather famous restaurant, the Nut Tree, located near Vacaville, California, was about halfway between my office in Brentwood and Blonien's office in Sacramento. We agreed to meet at that location and did so on June 23. From the outset, I liked this man. He was obviously extremely intelligent and very dedicated to "truth, justice, and the American way." He also possessed another character trait that I greatly appreciate, a terrific sense of humor. And he had heard our Med-fly Song on the radio and he liked it.

After feeling each other out, I presented him with an oral outline of the status of the situation and gave him copies of pertinent documents. He asked me why I was providing this information to the campaign. He stated that I probably wanted to be appointed as a judge. I told him no, this was far from the case; I only wanted to do what was right. If Bradley was the man I thought him to be, he should not head the state. He advised me that Bradley was refusing to make his tax returns public. This latter information later appeared in the *San Francisco Examiner* on July 22.

On June 24 I called Felix Stuckey. I suggested that a temporary executor be appointed in the case so that monies due could be collected. His reply was that he was traveling to Los Angeles to determine how he was going to be paid. He said our case would be a voluminous one and he wanted his jury trial.

On June 25 Stuckey filed a demand for jury trial. If I did not suspect an ulterior motive for the will contest before, I now not only suspected such, but I also knew it! First of all, this probate dispute would be determined by the court, not by a jury. Stuckey's obvious intent was not to have the case decided at all, but rather to delay, delay, delay, at least until after the November election.

16.

By August 1982 my apprehension that I might be physically harmed had largely subsided. My last contact with Bradley had been the receipt of his letter in May in which he said he would search for more documents; of course, three months later, he hadn't presented any documents. Now, I was fighting a will contest that, to me, was obviously designed to thwart my efforts to arrive at justice for Ruth Barrett and the deceased, John Bland. My feelings of apprehension, for the most part, had been replaced by those of anger. I was just plain mad. I had discussed this matter with Ruth Barrett many times over the months at each development, and she had agreed; even though she was herself African American, she would rather have the white guy in the office.

The general election was three months away. The winner would be governor. Bradley was far ahead of Deukmejian in all the polls.

The decision as to what to do next was an extremely tough one. If we were to go ahead from this point, it would certainly be a most time-consuming and expensive adventure. And an adventure it would surely be—not your run-of-the-mill lawsuit. But it would be something you could someday tell your grandkids about, should they happen to be interested.

Lawsuits should never be entered into lightly. Lawsuits are wars. They are nasty. They can exhaust the parties financially, physically, and emotionally. They are to be avoided if at all possible. They should be settled at the earliest possible date. Many cases are reluctantly settled because these projected exhaustive costs, financial and otherwise, will outweigh the benefits of proceeding. I have always been of the belief that just about any dispute can be settled if the parties and their attorneys are reasonable. It is only when reasonableness fails that the prospect of settlement also fails.

Before embarking on this avenue of approach, I consulted with several attorneys whom I had known and respected for some time. One was John Coker, a Pittsburg, California, attorney who was, and is, well known for his liberal views and was a mainstay in the Hispanic community. After a complete discussion of the facts of the case, John agreed I should proceed with a lawsuit. He also advised me that even though he had been a big Bradley supporter, after we talked and he examined the documents, he was withdrawing his support.

Another confidant was Tom Prelock from my old Bay Area law practice days. Tom was a huge man, at least six foot four, weighing in, I would estimate, at around three hundred pounds. He was an excellent trial lawyer practicing in El Cerrito. He was tough and gruff on the outside, intimidating as hell, but tender on the inside, although his inside did not often make an appearance. He took an immediate interest in the Bland matter. As an avid Republican, he had no objection if the facts were to come out during the course of the gubernatorial campaign. He offered to help me wherever and whenever I needed him.

I consulted with other attorneys. The opinions were unanimous. We had the facts to present to a jury, which would, by a preponderance of the evidence, lead to a judgment against Tom Bradley and possibly his wife, Ethel. The amount of the judgment would not be large unless we could be persuasive enough to convince the jury that they acted maliciously, in which case punitive damages would be a possibility. They also felt I was potentially in physical danger, but that this would cease as soon as a lawsuit was filed and open to public view.

17.

On August 6, 1982, at the Contra Costa County courthouse, I secured an order appointing Ruth Barrett as special administratrix of John Bland's estate. On the same date, I filed a motion to have the trial held at the earliest possible date, since it would be necessary to fight that battle to ensure that Ruth would be Bland's rightful heir. In my attached declaration, I alleged that the amount of the estate was $15,000, plus the disputed sum of more than $20,000 owed by Thomas Bradley, mayor of Los Angeles and gubernatorial candidate, and his wife, Ethel Bradley. I alleged it was necessary to speed up the proceeding, because the contestant, Louise Bland, was eighty-one years old; should she die, she would not be available as a material witness at trial. I also alleged that, in support of my motion to advance the case, Thomas Bradley would be a material witness in the case and, should he be elected governor, he would more than likely not be available to attend a trial, depositions, or any other proceedings.

With respect to the lawsuit against the Bradleys, there were many decisions to be made. First of all, in which county should the lawsuit be brought? A lawsuit may be properly filed in the county of residence of a defendant, or in the case of an alleged breach of contract, where the contract was entered into or to be performed.

Obviously, Los Angeles County was the most likely jurisdiction, since the Bradleys resided there, and they could argue that's where any dealings with Bland were initiated and consummated.

From my perspective, Los Angeles would be the worst. It was at least a seven-hour drive from northern Brentwood to LA. It would be awkward, to say the least, for me to handle a case down there, to make court appearances, attend depositions, and the like. Also, LA would not be a desirable location for us, when we considered the fact that Bradley lived there—he was mayor, for Pete's sake—and his constituency was there, which consisted of thousands of people. This would not be the best jury pool for our side should the case eventually be tried in court.

I would have loved to have had the case filed in my home court, Contra Costa County, because I was within a half-hour drive of the courthouse. However, there was no connection to the parties or the facts of the case to support my desire.

I did know that at the time that Bradley made this real estate deal with John Bland that Bland resided in San Mateo County. This might be enough to locate the case in that county, although I strongly suspected that if we filed there, Bradley's lawyers would move for a change of venue to LA County. San Mateo County is on the peninsula just south of San Francisco and north of the Silicon Valley.

San Mateo County was not my jurisdiction of choice in which to file a lawsuit, but it was the best I could do, and it was damned sure better than Los Angeles. It was only a ninety-minute drive, as opposed to seven hours.

The complaint was entitled *Ruth Barrett, Special Administratrix of the Estate of John Bland, Plaintiff, v. Thomas Bradley, Ethel Bradley, Does I through L, inclusive, Defendants.*

The complaint contained four causes of action, or theories, if you will. The first cause of action was for breach of contract. This alleged that there was a written agreement between the Bradleys and Bland that the Bradleys would purchase Bland's property for $25,000 and that, upon subsequent sale, the proceeds would be divided equally. Later, the property was sold to Bradley Ltd. for $110,000. Under the sale, Bradley received $23,000 and took back a note and deed of trust for $81,000. The note called for interest of 8 percent and monthly installment payments of $983 per month. Monthly payments to Bland continued up until the time of his death, whereupon Bradley denied there was any further obligation owing to Bland. As such, it was our contention that Bradley had breached the agreement.

The second cause of action was for fraud. Fraud, otherwise known as misrepresentation, consists of a statement that is knowingly or negligently made with the intent that another person will rely on the statement, and that the person relies on the statement and is harmed as a result. Bradley had told Bland that their agreement would be put into escrow and that they were to be partners in the property. These representations were false, and because he relied on them, Bland entered into the agreement. The fraud count went on to allege that Bradley failed to share the down payment, overcharged for expenses, prepared income tax returns for Bland that contained false information, and later denied any obligation owing to him. In addition to general damages—that is, actual monetary damages sustained—we alleged that punitive damages were applicable, to punish Bradley for his wrongful actions. We alleged a figure of two million dollars.

The third cause of action alleged that Bradley had breached his fiduciary duty to Bland. Bradley was an attorney. He had previously prepared Bland's will and was obviously self-dealing in the real estate transaction at hand. Bland was an eighty-year-old man, frail and ill. He was financially destitute and in dire need of help. These men were hardly equal and on even footings in any transaction. An attorney has the absolute duty to protect his client's interests at all times. Attorneys are bound by the highest standards of ethics. Our complaint alleged the following breaches of ethical duties by Tom Bradley:

a. Failed to advise Bland to seek independent counsel in subject transaction.
b. Possessed a proprietary interest in the lending institution from which he secured his money to purchase the property from Bland without so advising him.
c. Failed to deposit the agreement between the parties into the escrow.
d. Received an unwarranted credit on the sale of the property from the Blands to the Bradleys without disclosing the same to Bland.
e. On the sale of the property to Bradley Ltd., did not disclose to Bland that the principals of Bradley Ltd. were real estate brokers.
f. Failed to explain to Bland why monthly payments under the Bradley Ltd. note did commence for a year following the sale to them.
g. Failed to maintain a trust account for the transaction.
h. Commingled Bland's funds with his own.

i. Did not accurately share the proceeds of the sale with Bland.,

j. Provided Bland with a misleading accounting of funds.

k. By virtue of his position as an attorney and government official, had superior knowledge of the value of the property, which he failed to disclose to Bland.

l. Obtained an accountant, also a prominent political consultant, to prepare Bland's 1974 tax returns, which contain falsely stated facts, and wrongfully increased Bland's tax liability and decreased Bradley's.

m. Upon learning of Bland's death, denied owing any money to Bland or to his estate.

Again, in addition to a prayer for general damages, relief for an award of two million dollars in punitive damages was also sought.

The fourth cause of action alleged conspiracy, that both Tom and Ethel Bradley had conspired in the transaction with Bland, that they were aware of and had participated in the actions of the other. Punitive damages were also sought on this count.

18.

The complaint was filed with the State of California Superior Court, County of San Mateo, on August 10, 1982. It seemed unlikely that serving Bradley the papers would be an easy task. He was constantly on the road making his obligatory public appearances as a prelude to his day of reckoning in two months for the highest office in the state. I gave copies of the documents to a local process server, Andy, located in Pittsburg, California, to have Bradley served. Bradley's public appearance schedule was available and disclosed that he would be in Willows, California, on August 13. Andy traveled to Willows to attempt service. Willows is a town in North Central California with a population in 1982 of approximately 5,000. At 7:15 p.m., Andy arrived with his wife. A party was in progress. They mingled with the guests, his wife carrying the legal papers in her purse. Bradley and his wife, Ethel, arrived through a side door at eight thirty. He gave a short speech, pictures were taken, and they left. Andy told me he couldn't get anywhere near Bradley because of all of his bodyguards surrounding them at all times.

The filing of the lawsuit caught the immediate attention of the press. I do not know how many newspapers carried the story, but I do know it was in the *San Francisco Chronicle*, the *San Francisco Examiner*, the *Oakland Tribune,* and the *San Mateo Times Tribune.*

When contacted by reporters, I gave them my prepared statement: "I am not in a position at this time where I can talk about the case with the press for the reason that my client and I will be accused of filing for political reasons. All information concerning the matter may be found in two court filings. The information is there for those who care to read the documents on file." I provided the file case numbers. During each of the reporters' calls, I was invariably asked whether the case against Bradley had been filed for political reasons, which, of course, I denied.

Another attempt to serve the papers upon Bradley was later made in Concord, with the same result as that in Willows. It was impossible to get close enough to the man to serve him. On August 16 I sent a certified letter to the Bradleys. I enclosed copies of the complaint and requested they acknowledge receipt thereof, thereby accepting service.

I received a telephone call from an attorney from San Mateo County, who stated that he would be representing Tom and Ethel Bradley. He identified himself as Joe Cotchett. At the time I had no idea who Joe Cotchett was, but I was about to find out. I was to discover that I—this small-town, country, one-man show from Brentwood with a shared secretary—was about to go up against one of the premiere attorneys in the State of California, perhaps in the country, and his law firm, Cotchett, Dyer & Illston. The good news was that, no, the case would not be transferred to Los Angeles. The bad news was that my concerns about being outgunned legally were certainly to be realized.

In the 1980s there were no computers with which to check out opposing attorneys, or for that matter, anyone or anything else at all. Through several phone calls, I learned that Cotchett had already established himself as being a phenomenal trial lawyer, having won huge judgments in white-collar crime cases and jury verdicts of hundred of millions of dollars. I knew I had heard the name and later recognized it as being the same as the author of the law book on evidence that I regularly used. He and his firm would now be representing Tom Bradley and his wife.

On September 2, 1982, Cotchett filed the answer to our complaint on behalf of the Bradleys. The content of the answer was to basically deny our incriminating allegations. It was their contention that in late 1970, the Blands were about to lose their property to creditors, and that John Bland told Bradley he could have the property as a gift if he would pay off his creditors, but this offer of a gift was declined. Rather, they claimed that Bradley bought the property by paying off Bland's creditors and by giving him $5,000 in cash.

Bradley said he borrowed the money to buy the property. But he did not say he had paid himself back in full from the down payment received when he subsequently sold the property to Bradley Ltd. Also, there was no explanation why there was no escrow for the transaction between himself and Bland.

In the answer, Bradley's contention did totally change in one respect. Bradley for the first time admitted there was a continuing obligation owing to Bland under the note, even though he had previously denied this obligation in his letter to me of April 22, 1982. Actually, there was little choice but for him to admit this, because our complaint included a copy of Bradley's letter to Bland dated January 27, 1971, in which he had acknowledged this obligation. Now that he knew we had the proof, it had become impossible for Bradley to continue to deny it.

It was further Bradley's contention that he had not acted as an attorney in his transactions with Bland, that he had advised Bland to consult with his own attorney, and that Bland had stated that he had done so. He did admit he had formerly prepared wills for Bland as his attorney as a favor, but he had not charged him.

At this point I will interject that I personally reviewed an executed will that Bradley had prepared for Bland. The language therein was confusing, leading one around and around. One thing, however, was totally clear. The end result was that the will bequeathed Bland's entire estate to Bradley himself.

In their defense to our complaint, they contended that Ruth Barrett had no standing to bring the action in that "there is pending a disputed will contest concerning the handwritten will allegedly executed by John Bland eleven days before his death, and the contestant therein, John Bland's sister, claims that Ruth Barrett exercised undue and unfair influence over John Bland." In other words they were contending that Ruth was not yet established to be the person who could bring a lawsuit on behalf of Bland's estate.

It was clear that Cotchett was aware of the will contest that was proceeding in Contra Costa County.

Cotchett did not waste time. Along with his answer, he also served me with notices of depositions for Ruth Barrett and her husband, Nolan. He also set my deposition to produce all documents in our possession. Depositions were scheduled for September 13, 1982, at his office in San Mateo. I had a conflict on that date, and it was agreed that these depositions would proceed on the following day, September 14.

OK, so now we're into the case. Big-time! No backing down! Past the point of no return! Game time! Let's go!

19.

On September 14, 1982, I arrived at the law offices of Cotchett, Dyer & Illston in San Mateo for the scheduled depositions of Nolan and Ruth Barrett. In attendance for the Bradleys were Joe Cotchett and Susan Illston.

My first impression of Mr. Cotchett was that I could immediately see why he was respected by his peers, judges, and the general populace. He was fairly large of stature, totally self-assured. He was friendly, and it was obvious he would be liked by any jury. It was apparent that he was extremely intelligent, and in no short order, it was apparent that he was indeed an excellent attorney.

Also in attendance was his partner, Susan Illston. While also friendly, she was quite businesslike and was in full command of herself and the situation around her. She was a no-nonsense person. It was apparent to me that she, like her partner, was not to messed with without the certainty of ensuing consequences.

To give the reader a complete picture of the formidability of these two attorneys, we would have to jump ahead some thirty years, get on a computer, and google them.

Today Mr. Cotchett is renowned as one of the foremost trial law-yers in the country. He has been repeatedly named as one of the most influential lawyers in the nation. He has attained verdicts in the billions of dollars. The accolades go on and on.

Susan Illston, herself an excellent attorney, was unanimously rec-ommended by Senators Diane Feinstein and Barbara Boxer and was appointed federal judge by President Clinton in 1995. It has been observed that she has the makings of a fine US Supreme Court Justice.

And so, back thirty years ago, we sat in their offices, the court re-porter at the ready.

First up was Ruth's quiet and unassuming husband, Nolan Barrett. His deposition was short, as he didn't really know much about any of the facts of the case. His testimony was that he was retired from the military and that he ran a grocery/liquor store in San Francisco until 1981. He now ran a catering truck and had a fruit stand. He had met John Bland in 1979. A few months prior to his death, Bland had called Ruth, Nolan's wife, to pick him up because he "didn't have nobody to look after him. He didn't have no food or like that. And he just needed somebody to, you know, take care of him." Ruth and Nolan had taken care of Bland, providing him with food and shelter. Over the months he and Bland would discuss "this and that." Bland had told him to stay on Ruth to get a lawyer to have his will drawn. He wanted Ruth to get what he had "be-cause none of his relatives ever did nothing for him." Nolan either did not know or could not recall any details of any dealings with Bradley that might have been related to him. When asked the state of John Bland's health when he was living with the Barretts, Nolan responded, "Well, it couldn't have been too good, because he died."

Nolan recalled that he had previously met some of John's acquaintances, but he couldn't remember their names, "but right now I couldn't recall your name [Cotchett] or hers [Illston] either."

"So, you don't remember?" Cotchett asked.

"I just told you," Nolan responded. "I can't remember her name [indicating Ms. Illston]. She told me two minutes ago."

Nolan was asked about any conversations he may have had with his wife, Ruth, regarding John Bland. "I can't tell you the conversation we had. Me and my wife talk together all of the time, when we're talking."

"Did your wife ever mention any other wills to you, besides Mr. Bland's will?"

"No. Because I don't even have that myself."

"What's that?" asked Cotchett.

"No, because I don't even have any myself."

"You don't have any yourself?"

"Not yet, I'm not planning on going now."

Cotchett asked Nolan whether Ruth had ever discussed any of the details of the pending lawsuit. He responded, "No. If I knew that, I wouldn't be sitting here talking. I'd be somewhere else."

During the course of his deposition, Nolan did say that Bland told him he did not get all that he was supposed to get from Bradley.

And finally, Cotchett asked, "Other than Mr. Allen, have you talked to any other lawyers about this lawsuit?"

"No," Nolan replied. "In fact, I haven't talked to nobody about nothing. Like I say, I don't talk that much."

And so concluded the deposition of Nolan Barrett.

20.

After a break, the deposition of Ruth Barrett commenced.

She had worked in the same grocery/liquor store as had Nolan and had recently been engaged in home care. She worked for Upjohn Health Care and Quality Home Care and was on call when these companies needed her to care for persons in their homes.

She testified she had met John Bland in the late fifties at a friend's beauty shop. She didn't see him again until the late seventies, meeting him through a mutual friend. They hit it off famously because they both liked to fish. The California Delta provides striped bass, black bass, sturgeon, catfish, and, to a lesser extent, salmon. One of their favorite spots was off Five Mile Road, which is near Stockton, California. For two years or so, John and his wife, Velma, until her death in 1980, were constant visitors.

After Velma's death John took up with at least two other women. Each time he told Ruth he was going to get married. The experiences with these women turned out to be disastrous for him, because each of them took his money; one of them even physically beat him up. He changed his will several times during this two-year time period, since his feelings would diminish as his funds were depleted, and as he suffered both mental and physical abuse. During all of this, he was in contact with Ruth. Ruth was his mentor.

In January 1982, Bland called Ruth and asked her if she would come get him. He was so destitute that he had no food. When she picked him up, all he had were pajamas, a robe, and some shoes. He gave Ruth a box full of papers, telling her that Tom Bradley had cheated him, that the papers in the box would prove this, and that he wanted her to get a lawyer for him.

Later that month John was hospitalized for nine days, but his health did improve, and he was released. He and Ruth appeared at my office, desiring a power of attorney for Ruth so she could collect the money in the bank account for him and pay some of his bills. I had prepared the document at his request.

Ruth and Nolan took care of John before he died in March. At no charge to him, they provided room, food, and all other necessities, plus his medical equipment. All the while John incessantly told Ruth to take the box of papers to an attorney. At ten o'clock on the night of March 5, 1982, John was running a temperature of a hundred and four. He was transported to the hospital by ambulance. There, he told Ruth, as she was feeding him some ice cream, to look in the box. She told him to take it easy, that he wasn't going to die. Unfortunately, he did. Ruth and Nolan paid his funeral expenses.

Approximately a week after John's death, Ruth was cleaning up his room when she looked in the box. A document in John's handwriting lay on top. It was his holographic will, dated February 22, 1982. The terms of this will provided for his entire estate to go to Ruth.

Cotchett referred Ruth to the will contest that had been filed in the Contra Costa County court. He had the documents from that case and began to grill her on the petition to have her appointed special administratrix. He asked her what facts she possessed to allege that "it was also necessary that action be commenced against the Bradleys to recover sums due and owing the estate, in that funds may well be depleted by expenditures incurred by them in the upcoming gubernatorial race." Cotchett and Ruth went "round and round" with this one. Ruth handled this very well, eventually stating that "if they are not paying money they owe John Bland, as far as I am concerned, they are spending money that belongs to John Bland, whether it's gubernatorial or grocery bill. They are holding money that belongs to John Bland."

What followed next was a lengthy, often contentious, examination of Ruth as to the basis of her lawsuit. Cotchett wanted all facts upon which Ruth based each of the allegations against Bradley. He asked what facts she had upon which to base the allegation that "Bradley failed to share the down payment received from the sale of the property to Bradley Ltd. with John Bland." He asked what facts Ruth possessed to claim that Bradley had caused tax returns to be filed for Bland that contained false information. He asked about how the claim for damages of "in excess of $20,000" had been determined; what facts she had to support the allegation that Bradley and Bland were partners; what facts she had to support the allegation that Bradley made false representations to Bland, knowing them to be false; and what she had to show that Bradley failed to advise Bland to seek the advice of his own attorney before making the deal with Bradley.

After hours of examination by Mr. Cotchett, Ruth was unable to pinpoint with accuracy the precise evidence to show that Bradley had done what he was alleged to have done.

Cotchett: You see, Mrs. Barrett, you don't understand. We're going to be here a very long time unless you can tell me. We have to list them. There are very serious charges you have made here.

Ruth: Right. And very serious things done. So, I can't point line for line for you.

Cotchett: Are those the documents?

Ruth: I can't say this is the only ones that it's in, and then when we get to something and it has something else in there, then I would be having to explain why. I say I went through the whole thing. I am not an attorney and I am not an accountant; but from what I can read, this is where my information came from.

Cotchett: From these four documents?

Barrett: All the documents.

Cotchett: No you can't, ma'am—you have to tell me all the—

Allen: Plus information from the parties, plus other information that can be gleaned from the entire file.

The examination went on and on along these lines for hours. Ms. Illston would interject her own questions into the fray, which I tolerated for a while. At one point I had to request that only one of them ask the questions. The bottom line here was that Ruth Barrett was not an attorney, and she was not an accountant. At trial the facts of the case would come out, not only through Ruth, but also through others, accountants, appraisers, and Bradley himself, when I put him on the witness stand.

21.

At the conclusion of the depositions, after working hours, Susan Illston went through the documents in the boxes while Joe Cotchett and I discussed the case. He was aware of no less than eight wills that had been written and prepared on behalf of John Bland. One was a 1971 will prepared for him by Tom Bradley in which Bland left everything he had to Bradley. Cotchett stated there was now an admission that Bradley owed $16,000 in the matter and was anxious to settle the case. I said I could not advise a settlement until I was convinced Bradley had no connection with Bradley Ltd., the purchaser of the Moreno property, and that he had not received any kickbacks. I needed more information and discovery of more documents, and it would also be necessary to take Mr. Bradley's deposition.

I was told this case was screwing up Bradley's campaign for governor in that he had to fly in on a private plane to confer with his attorney, thereby missing political appointments. I was also advised that the issue of possible welfare fraud could cause the largest problem politically for Bradley.

Cotchett told me that his law firm was fully aware of the will contest now proceeding in the Contra Costa County courts and that our side would eventually prevail in that matter.

Any further efforts to settle the case were not pursued by either side.

On September 17, 1982, Joe Cotchett sent me a letter providing what he considered to be proof of the fact that Tom Bradley had absolutely no connection with Bradley Ltd. He provided copies of the agreement of limited partnership, certificate of limited partnership, and amendments that had been recorded in Orange and Riverside Counties. He went on to express his "surprise" that I had not myself secured these documents. In retrospect he was probably right on this one. He further expressed his displeasure that I had not responded to Bradley's letter of May 8, 1982, and did not provide Bradley with information and documents he claimed that he could not locate. Well, with respect to that assertion, it was quite unlikely that Bradley could not locate his documents; he was just fishing to see what we had. The more he knew that we had, the more he would be forced to admit. This, as we've seen, turned out to be exactly the case when he at first denied any obligation to Bland, but later, after he was confronted with his own letter, admitted the obligation. Cotchett went on to say that had I responded to Bradley, any uncertainties could have been resolved and possibly an escrow arranged. A good defense is a good offense. Trial lawyers do what they can to take the offensive. Was it possible that they were attempting to make me the bad guy by attacking my integrity and motives in the handling of this case?

On September 20 Felix Stuckey and I appeared at the Contra Costa County Courthouse, the Honorable Max Wilcox Jr. presiding.

Fortunately for us, Wilcox ruled that the will contest matter was advanced for trial to December 6, 1982.

On September 21 I sent a letter to Mr. Cotchett advising that it would be difficult to settle the case, because we had alleged that Bradley had defrauded Bland and had breached his fiduciary duty to him, but Bradley had totally denied these allegations. Although I did not tell Cotchett, I was pissed that the will contest filed by Attorney Stuckey remained. I agreed to comply with Cotchett's request that Bradley's deposition be taken at the earliest possible date at the location of their choice.

By this time I had received calls from the Associated Press, the *Sacramento Bee,* and Channel Two News out of Oakland. To each I read my prepared statement, which in essence referred them to the court records.

On September 28 I received a letter from Mr. Cotchett. His language had hardened considerably. He maintained their position that Bradley had not committed any fraud nor had he breached any fiduciary duty. He stated that the Bradleys went out of their way to assist John Bland; that they had provided a means for him to save his property from foreclosure; and that because of their efforts, Mr. Bland not only did not lose his property, but was also paid over $40,700 by the time of his death. Cotchett stated that John Bland was a man quick to accuse and intemperate of language and that his claims were baseless. His stories were utterly invalid, Cotchett claimed. He further suggested that over the years, Bland tried to take advantage of Tom and Ethel Bradley. He added that had I responded to Bradley's letter of inquiry to me, I might have discovered this myself. He claimed he found it impossible to understand my treatment of these serious allegations, that I had no evidence whatsoever to show any wrongdoing on Bradley's part. He demanded I withdraw the charges (dismiss the complaint). He concluded his letter by stating that Bradley should not be forced to continue in a case that bore no merit.

There was no offer to settle the case, only a demand to drop the case in its entirety.

On September 29 I filed and served a notice for them to produce documents, which demanded that Bradley, through his attorneys, produce any and all documents that could in any way be construed to be involved in our case. All in all, thirty-two demands were contained in the notice. I also prepared and served notices to take Tom and Ethel's depositions on October 25. As a convenience to their side, the depositions would take place in Los Angeles at the LA County Bar Association office.

I also scheduled the deposition of Louise Smith in the Contra Costa County will contest case and served Felix Stuckey with those documents. I set her deposition for the same date and location as Bradley's deposition, as a convenience to myself.

I began my inquiry into the makeup of the San Mateo County Superior Court bench. Judges, like everyone else, have political leanings. Those judges who were not originally seated by virtue of an election were appointed by the governor of California. Most are. Many of the seated judges were appointed by Jerry Brown. As such, the bench was quite liberal, as was evident from his appointment of Rose Bird as chief justice of the California Supreme Court. Through my attorney friends, I located a friendly deputy district attorney in San Mateo County who provided me with a description, from his point of view, of each and every judge in that county. He advised me that generally the bench was Democratic, with some of them belonging to a strong Democratic clique. Without identifying each judge with the characteristics provided, I received information such as, "loner, liberal, no-nonsense, tough on violent crime, watch out, very active Democrat behind the scenes, meticulous, wishy-washy, very active Democratic wife, borders on incompetence, well respected, likeable, wimp, no balls, rules abruptly, independent, Republican, judge maker, political hack, good man, fair, independent." Seven of the judges were reportedly members of the Democratic clique.

I was further advised that Joe Cotchett was on a first-name basis with Governor Jerry Brown and was responsible for, or at least had a say in, judicial appointments in San Mateo County. Reportedly, many of the judges there treated Cotchett with deference.

The evening of September 29, Max and I sat down in front of the TV to watch the debate between Bradley and Deukmejian. The election was just over a month away.

22.

The next few days, I was bombarded by the press. Channel 2 News wanted to interview me. I declined, reading them my prepared statement. The reporter advised me she had interviewed Joe Cotchett and was in the process of getting an interview from Bradley. She told me Cotchett had told her the lawsuit was frivolous and politically motivated. Not knowing whether or not Cotchett had told her that, I still declined.

On October 4 she called back and told me Cotchett had been on camera and they would hold off airing until they had the whole story. If I continued to refuse an interview, they would air what they had, including Cotchett's statement. She told me that, not only had Cotchett labeled the suit frivolous and politically motivated, but he had also told her that Bradley had done a little will for Bland at no charge, that he had worked for free in the real estate matter, and that Ruth Barrett had wrongfully coerced Bland to change his will several days before his death.

With Ruth's concurrence I now agreed to the interview. The next day the reporter, Betty Anbruno, appeared at my office. Word somehow got around, and Bob Taylor of the *Sacramento Union* was also there, as was a representative from our local *Brentwood News*.

On October 6 a lengthy story appeared on the front page of the *Sacramento Union,* as well as in other newspapers on or about that date.

23.

That night Max and I watched Channel 2 News. When interviewed, Cotchett said exactly what the reporter earlier had told me he had said.

Late in the day of October 6, I received a call from a reporter by the name of Jeff Reybin, who was with the *Sacramento Bee*. He posed several questions, which I answered. He asked if I thought Bradley was behind the will contest in Contra Costa County. I declined to answer that one.

On October 7 nothing happened. I received absolutely no telephone calls regarding the case. The only thing I learned that day was that the polls showed Bradley had increased his lead over Deukmejian by fourteen points, according to the *Sacramento Bee*. The *Bee* also reported that Bradley himself had labeled the Bland action as politically motivated.

On October 8 I received a call from Attorney Illston saying Bradley would only be available for his deposition at 8:00 a.m. for two hours on October 12. I advised her I had a previous appearance scheduled in federal court that morning and could not accommodate that date. I also advised her that I needed at least six hours for this deposition. There was a lot to be covered. I advised her of many of my available dates and told her I would accommodate Mr. Bradley by conducting the deposition at the location of his choosing so long as it was within a reasonable driving distance or close to an airport.

Following a series of rather heated exchanges, we finally agreed that Mr. Bradley's deposition would occur at 8:00 a.m. Saturday, October 23, 1982, at the mayor's office, city hall, Los Angeles, California.

My attorney buddy, Tom Prelock, the guy as physically big as Tom Bradley, the excellent criminal trial lawyer and avid Republican, was closely following my two cases. He was a great listening post for me and often advanced his opinions and recommendations. When he heard I was about to take Bradley's deposition, he really wanted to be there. My thought was, *what the hell, why not.* Two heads are better than one. Also, since Bradley was known to have bodyguards, I might as well appear with one of my own. I had no idea if Prelock could fight, but I did not believe anybody with any sense would even want to attempt to find out. So, the day before the deposition, I associated him in as co-counsel. We bought our plane tickets and were ready to go.

24.

On October 22, 1982, the *Los Angeles Times* ran a front-page story on the race for governor. It mentioned nothing about the Bland matters, but it did contain one gem of information about Bradley that would assist me in our upcoming confrontation. It was said that Bradley apparently conducted business in the same manner as a high-stakes poker player. He was smooth and slick, and one didn't know what he was thinking. He was a listener more than a talker. Being a poker player myself, I knew he would be even more formidable than I had originally thought.

That day Tom Prelock and I flew to Los Angeles. We decided to travel the day prior to the deposition so we would be bright-eyed and bushy-tailed in the morning. In view of the seriousness of the matter, we decided it wise to forgo cocktails that evening. There would be plenty of time for that later. We talked about the case and about all that we knew about Bradley and retired early.

The next day at eight, we arrived at city hall. It was just like the pictures we had seen; after all, it was a fairly famous building.

We were greeted by two larger, armed gentlemen. After frisking us they led us through a maze of hallways that eventually took us into the office of the mayor. Bradley's office was beautiful. It was huge, luxuriously furnished with many appointments, accents, and photographs. Bradley was there, with both Joe Cotchett and Susan Illston. Introductions went around, and there stood the mayor. Bradley was even more imposing than that depicted in his photographs. Dressed in a sharp suit and tie, he looked as though he had just dropped in from a movie set. Surprisingly, for such a large man, his moves were catlike. He shook hands as though he and I had been best of friends for years. He was truly gracious when he offered coffee to us all and personally served it from his silver tea set.

There were two court reporters in attendance. As the deposing attorney, I was obliged to provide a court reporter. Their side apparently thought they should have their own. After being sworn in by both court reporters, the deposition of Thomas Bradley commenced at 8:30 a.m.

He had attended public schools in Los Angeles, then UCLA for three years, from 1937 to 1940. He then joined the LA Police Department, where he remained for twenty-one years. He attended Southwestern University Law School in the evenings and passed the California bar exam in 1956. He was first elected to the city council in 1963.

I decided I would not waste any time getting to the meat of why we were there.

Q: I have read an account of your comment, at least one of your comments on this case, wherein it is alleged that you have said that it is politically motivated. Did you make that statement?

A: Yes.

Q: Do you have any facts to base that statement—

A: Just my speculation based upon the nature of the manner in which it has been handled and reported to the press. Instead of serving me with papers, the press was notified. I can think of no motivation other than political in nature for that kind of approach to handling a lawsuit. Another reason is that one of the reporters told me that Ruth Barrett had indicated to him when he interviewed her that she had approached the Deukmejian people and offered to help his campaign.

He stated this had occurred two or three years ago, but he could not remember the reporter's name, and he wasn't sure if he was with the *Sacramento Bee* or the *Sacramento Union*.

He testified that he had met John Bland forty years previously. He would see him occasionally at family functions, although he could not recall where or when. He didn't know at which family member's place he had seen him, nor did he know how many people were in his family.

When asked whether he, as an attorney, had ever represented Bland, he replied, "No. The only thing I ever did for him was at his request to prepare a will for him."

Bradley did not recall Bland's 1965 letter to him asking for his help.

He stated that in December 1970, Bland approached him and offered to give him the property if his debts approximating $25,000 would be paid off. Bland told Bradley that the property was worth $100,000. Bradley and his wife viewed the property, and without checking its value or the encumbrances against the property, made the deal with Bland.

At nine o'clock Bradley excused himself because he had a scheduled radio appearance pertaining to the election, but said he would be back at ten thirty.

During the break Tom Prelock and I conferred. We agreed Bradley was one shrewd son of a bitch, but that he could be taken down by a slow, methodical examination. Hit him from different angles, and we could get to him. We were in that high-stakes poker game with him. As in a poker game, be incessant; hit him with your best shots, back down when you think you will lose, lie low, set him up, and then strike hard when you know you've got him.

At 10:25 a.m. the deposition continued. In response to questioning, Bradley testified that he knew absolutely nothing about the area in which the property was located, knew nothing about development plans that included a dam and a recreational lake until Bland told him about it.

Bradley said that, upon viewing the property with his wife, Ethel, he couldn't remember whether or not he began to negotiate with Bland's creditors even before he made any deal with Bland. But he said he commenced these negotiations within a week of seeing the property. He stated he did nothing to check out the property, but he knew that "it easily was worth the amount of money which he had asked for [$25,000], so there wasn't any doubt about that."

He later stated that he made the agreement with Bland after he had completed the negotiations with the lienholders. He had prepared the agreement at his office.

Q: What was your next contact with Bland? Did you call him or did he call you?

A: Let's see, after preparing the agreement, as I recall, the next conversation I had with him was to ask that he—oh, I had asked him to review that with his lawyer and to then tell me whether or not there was any problem with the agreement, and he called me back, to tell me that he had checked with his lawyer, that it was OK.

Bradley then testified that, when he mailed the agreement to Bland, there was a cover letter that contained the words, "Done in haste because it was to be delivered to escrow." I asked what he meant by that.

A: The actual preparation was done prior to the close of escrow.

Q: Did you mean that you wanted to get the agreement into the escrow?

A: No. No. There was never any discussion about including that in escrow.

He testified at first that he had no contact with Bland between the time of his viewing the property and his sending the agreement to him for signature. He subsequently changed his testimony.

Question by Allen: Excuse me. I just did not understand. I still don't understand what you meant by saying, "Done in haste because it was to be delivered at close of escrow."

A. The note.

Q. The note itself—

A. Yes.

Q. —was to be delivered at close of escrow?

A. No. The note was done in haste.

Q. Right. I understand that. But I don't understand what you mean by saying, "Done in haste because it was to be delivered at close of escrow."

Mr. Cotchett: I don't understand your question.

Mr. Allen: I don't understand what that sentence means.

Mr. Cotchett: He just explained it.

The Witness (Bradley): This agreement was to be completed by then.

Q. By the close of escrow?

A. Right. Prior to the close of escrow.

Q. But it wasn't your intent to put the agreement into escrow, was it?

A. Never. We had never discussed putting that into escrow.

Q. Then why was it important to have it done before close of escrow?

Mr. Cotchett: Well, that is argumentative, and why was it—

Mr. Allen: No, it hasn't—it hasn't been answered.

Mr. Cotchett: No. No.

The Witness: That was our understanding—

Mr. Cotchett: Wait. I'm objecting to the form of the question. You are saying why wasn't it. He testified the simple fact, it was their understanding, as I understand, it was not to go into escrow. Right?

The Witness: That is true.

Mr. Cotchett: OK.

Q: Then why make the statement, "Done in haste because it was to be delivered at close of escrow."

Mr. Cotchett: It was very simple. They had to have it signed before they could close escrow. They wanted to have an agreement before the escrow closed.

Q: For what legal purpose? Was there a legal purpose?

A: It was our understanding, I wanted that completed before the escrow on the whole matter closed.

Q: Why?

Mr. Cotchett: Wait. Wait. What are you asking why? I mean we are here to get the facts.

Mr. Allen: That's right. I'm just trying to find out what his position is.

We went around and around this for at least five more minutes. I never did get an answer. It was clear to me that Bradley, by his own admission, did not ever intend that their true agreement be put into escrow. He did not want any evidence that this agreement ever existed. How else would he be able to wrongfully take the money after Bland should die?

At a later point during the deposition, the dialogue between Mr. Cotchett and myself became quite heated.

Q (to Bradley): Do you remember if he [Bland] ever called you during that period of time [referring to the time between Bradley's purchase and the time of the sale to Bradley Ltd.] inquiring as to what was happening with the property?

A: I know we talked about it.

Mr. Cotchett: Counsel, here is a letter in the file Mayor Bradley wrote to him—

Mr. Allen: What was the date?

Mr. Cotchett: —what was going on.

Mr. Allen: What is the date?

Mr. Cotchett: Is there a date on there, Mayor?

Mr. Bradley: No, there is no date on this.

Mr. Cotchett: Is that an example of your writing—John, tell him—

Mr. Allen: Counsel, let me take the deposition.

Mr. Cotchett: Sure. I'm trying to tell you we have certain documents here that come out of your files. We are not here to—we are here to get the facts.

Mr. Allen: That's fine. I'm asking for his recollection. If I want to produce documents, Counsel, I'll do that. Thank you. I appreciate that.

Mr. Cotchett: Fine. What I'm saying is you are wasting a lot of time screwing around here with a lot of time between each question.

Mr. Allen: Counsel, I appreciate your comments. If you would let me go ahead with my deposition, I'd appreciate it.

Mr. Cotchett: Fine. If you've got a question, ask it.

Mr. Allen: Thank you very much.

And later, to Bradley:

Q: Did you ever consider at this time that you were a partner with the Blands in this property?

A: No. I considered that Bland was going to share in the net proceeds that came out of this sale. The sale to Bradley Ltd. provided cash to pay off Bradley's loan to his Bank and for a Note to Bradley for $81,000. It also provided that payments on the Note would not commence for a year.

He did not consult with Bland because "The property had been transferred to me and my wife. He was not part of that sale."

Q: You didn't think it was appropriate to check with Mr. Bland to see if this deal was OK with him?

A: There was no understanding, no agreement, no request that it be done.

Bradley, in response to my questions, testified that in 1974, he prepared an accounting and sent it to John Bland to provide him with a summary of the sale, the amount of money to be paid, when it was to start, the monthly payments, and an accounting of expenses which Bradley had paid, amounts he had been reimbursed and for which he expected reimbursement.

Q: So, you deducted all taxes, interest payments, payments on principal on your note and all expenses ever incurred by yourself on the property?

A: That is correct.

Q: Is it true that you are (were) into the property for nothing?

A: No, I have not been fully reimbursed.

Q: What were you not reimbursed for?

A: The $1,500 which I gave him because he was short, he needed some money.

Bradley testified that in addition to this $1,500, there was $916, which he had put into the escrow and $149 of out-of-pocket expenses. He claimed an additional $1,000. Bradley amortized the total figure over a period of ten years and then deducted the sum of $76 per month from the amount that he sent to Bland.

He stated that although monthly payments by Bradley Ltd. were not to commence for a year after the sale, Bradley Ltd. did give Bland the sum of $5,000 as advanced interest on the loan.

I showed Bradley the letter dated February 28, 1979, from Bland to Maggie, who was Ethel Bradley's sister; he stated he had never seen it. At that point, as that letter was unsigned, there ensued a discussion as to whether it had been written by John Bland or not. This was the letter in which Bland expressed his extreme sorrow that Bradley would not cosign for a $5,000 loan to keep him going.

Q: In about the year 1979, did John Bland ask for you to help him get $5,000?

A: He did at one time ask me to help arrange a loan at the bank for $5,000.

Q: Did you accommodate him and make an effort to help him get a loan?

A: The bank felt that they could lend him $3,000 if I would guarantee its repayment out of his regular portion of the money coming from Bradley Ltd. They felt that if they loaned him $5,000 that the monthly payment would be so great that he would not have sufficient money left and it would not be a reasonable loan. I indicated that to Bland and he declined to take the $3,000 loan so he got none.

Tom Prelock and I glanced at each other upon that response. Sure, the bank would not accept an application for a $5,000 loan when it was to be cosigned by the mayor of Los Angeles. Right! And certainly they would not do so when the mayor was also a founder of and shareholder of the bank. Right! And Bland, as destitute as he was, would turn down a loan because it was only $3,000. Right!

I then referred Bradley to his letter to Bland dated March 13, 1979, in which he expressed his indignation with Bland.

Q: It starts off by saying, I believe, "I'm shocked and surprised at some accusations". Do you remember what those accusations were?

A: I was a part of Bradley Ltd., that he had not received–something to do with interest owed.

Q: In that letter you state that you are going to drop the $76 a month deduction from his one-half; is that right?

A: Yes.

Q: Why did you do that?

A: In this letter I explained to him all of the responses to his statements and I said that we had operated in good faith all along and that I didn't want to be a party to an arrangement where he expressed that kind of dissatisfaction and I was foregoing any further reimbursement to which I was entitled.

Q: You do say in the letter, "I would rather lose this $76 monthly payment obligation than continue an arrangement with a partner who is so unhappy that he would raise accusations that I listed on the first two pages of this letter."

A: Yes.

Q: You did consider him as a partner; is that right?

Mr. Cotchett: In a legal sense?

Mr. Bradley: No.

Mr. Allen: In any sense?

Mr. Bradley: Not in a legal sense.

I then went back in time to Bland's attempt to go on welfare. Bradley admitted that Bland had sent him the letter dated February 25, 1971, from the welfare department denying benefits because they showed that he owned the Moreno property. Bradley further admitted to sending his letter of explanation back to the welfare department.

Q: You are telling them in that letter, I believe, and correct me if I'm wrong, that you have paid or John Bland has been paid $5,000 in cash but no cash is left to John Bland.

A: At that point, that's right.

Q: At that point. Did you tell the welfare department that he had the remaining one-half interest in the proceeds of the property upon subsequent sale?

A: They received all of the forms, including escrow papers, the agreement between me and Mr. Bland, and some other forms which the department had sent to Mr. Bland.

Q: Did you say that you sent the agreement between you and Bland to the welfare department?

A: Yes.

Q: Do you have any correspondence or evidence to show us that you did in fact send this agreement to the Welfare Department?

A: No.

Bradley denied that the purpose of the welfare department's letter was to indicate that they would deny welfare to Bland if they knew that Bland had an ownership interest in the property. He stated that their letter was requesting information as to whether or not he still owned the property, and if he had sold it, if he had informed them of the proceeds.

The escrow papers sent to the department, of course, did not show that Bland had any interest whatsoever. Their true agreement had not gone into the escrow.

Did Bradley, in truth, send a copy of his agreement with Bland to the department? The reader can make his own decision on this one. And I have a bridge to sell you.

I then jumped to 1975, asking Mr. Bradley about his handling of Bland's 1974 tax returns. Bradley had Jules Glazer prepare the returns. Glazer was a CPA who handled Bradley's personal accounts, as well as many of his political accounts. Bradley stated that he paid Bland's taxes that year, totaling about a thousand dollars, and that he did so because Bland had no money.

Bradley testified that Bland's tax return attributed one-half of the gross sale price to Bland and that one-half of the expenses were also attributed to Bland. The returns also falsely showed that Bland had acquired the property in 1971. Bradley stated that he did not know why the return showed the 1971 date.

Next, I asked Bradley about my initial letters to him dated March 12 and April 9, 1982 and his responsive letter dated April 22.

Q: Would you tell me what you meant by the fourth paragraph, starting with the word "although," which states: "Although, by the terms of our agreement, there was no further obligation to Mr. Bland following the sale of the land in 1974, I have sent him half of the money I received."

A: From the outset of the discussions, Mr. Bland had indicated that he—if we would pay off those obligations, that he would deed that land to us and that there would be no further obligations. That was his position on the matter. I indicated to him that I would not take the property under those circumstances. I would give him half of the net proceeds after all expenses were paid, after we were able to sell the land.

Q: As of April 22, 1982, did you in fact have an obligation to Mr. Bland or to his estate?

A: That I'm not sure—was not sure of at that point. In our discussions, he did not—after his death—this was during his lifetime that these payments were to be made for his representation to me. After his death, until there was some clear indication by a subsequent will or an action by the Court, there was no legal obligation.

Q: At the time that you sent me this letter, were you of the opinion that your agreement with Bland was still valid?

A: I don't know.

Q: Did you think it expired with his death?

A: Yes, possible. If there was some subsequent action by will or otherwise that would have bound me according to the Court, I would not have any reservation about that. But in the absence of that, it was not clear.

Q: Aren't you, in essence, telling me in your letter that you have no obligation to Bland at all?

Mr. Cotchett interposed an objection.

Q: Are you aware as an attorney that an obligation to a person does not expire with his death?

A: The reason that I have some reservations about responding to your question, that could have changed by virtue of a will. That could have been changed by a subsequent will. So, until I know what that subsequent will said, I am not able to answer.

I looked over at Tom Prelock; he had a faint smile on his face.

Further questioning revealed that Bradley, in his negotiations with Bland's creditors to reduce their liens, had typed "legal matter" at the top of the letter and had signed his name, with the words "attorney at law" on the bottom.

Q: You were not representing John Bland as an attorney—

A: No.

Q: —in that letter?

A: No, I was not.

Q: Were you representing yourself?

Bradley then proceeded to bob and weave to all further questions along these lines. This line of questioning was also interesting to me because Bradley had only practiced law from 1961 to 1963.

The deposition also revealed that Tom Bradley had not signed the promissory note for the $25,000 with his bank. Only Ethel had signed, and Bradley testified he did not know why this was the case.

I have earlier told you about the will that Bradley prepared for Bland in 1971. Bradley also prepared one for Velma. Whether Bradley was licensed by the California State Bar of California to practice law in 1971, I do not know. Their website does not provide this information, and I make no representation as to whether or not he was actively licensed.

Bradley testified that, yes, he had prepared these wills for them. At their request Bradley was named executor. He stated that under the provisions of the will, all of their household furniture and personal effects were to go to himself to dispose of as he saw fit. The will provided that should John or Velma own any real estate at the time of their death, that Bradley and his wife, Ethel, were to get a life estate therein. Finally, the wills provided that the residue of the estate (meaning anything else) was to be given to Tom and Ethel Bradley.

In response to questioning, Bradley testified that at the time he prepared these wills, Bland's Moreno property was to be transferred to the Bradleys, and he also knew that the Blands owned no other property. Therefore, Bradley acknowledged he would get anything and everything that the Blands owned.

Q: Had Bland sold the [Moreno] property to you and had there been money owing under the promissory note, that money would have gone to you and your wife?

A: Yes.

As to his wife, Ethel's, involvement in the dealings with Bland, Bradley testified that she did not know everything that had transpired. She was aware of the terms of the sale of the property to Bradley Ltd.

On the advice of his attorney, Bradley refused to answer questions relating to the previous lawsuit involving his nephews and himself.

Bradley admitted he had talked to Attorney Felix Stuckey. Bradley testified that Stuckey's client, Louise Smith, had requested that Bradley call Stuckey to get information pertaining to our will contest in Contra Costa County.

Bradley further testified that he had no facts upon which to base his allegation contained in his answer to the complaint that Ruth Barrett ever exercised undue influence over John Bland, nor was he aware of the *Sacramento Union* article's comment that Barrett may or may not have been stealing money from Bland.

It was late when the deposition concluded. I would have to carefully review the transcript when it became available. After all, other than Bradley, I really had no other witnesses who would be able to testify at trial as to what had occurred over these years. Did I, and would I, have enough now that I had Bradley's deposition, to be able to make our case against him in front of a jury? I was fairly sure he would be my first witness at trial after jury selection and opening statements. I would have to establish our case through him. Sure, I would bring in an accountant, a real estate appraiser, and possibly others, but my main witness, who could explain all the intricate details in all of the events, was John Bland, and, most unfortunately, he was unable to testify because he was dead.

25.

Meanwhile, serious issues had arisen with Felix Stuckey in the will contest case. During a telephone conversation on October 21, since I had not heard from him, I asked if Louise Smith's deposition was still on for October 25 in Los Angeles. He advised me that he still did not know who was going to pay his expenses. He further told me that Louise had never returned his call, and he was again attempting to contact her. He stated that the deposition might have to be continued, but he would attempt to salvage the October 25 date. He said he would let me know.

Stuckey did not call back. Carole, my secretary, called his office and was told he was busy. She told his secretary that the deposition would go ahead for October 25, and, if they did not appear, I would take the matter up with the court. She also told them that the deposition could be held at Louise's home, if that would be helpful.

Stuckey sent me a letter dated October 22 in which he stated that Louise was eighty-one years old and largely confined to a wheelchair. She simply did not feel fit enough to attend a deposition. However, I did not receive this letter until after October 25, so on that date, I was once again in LA for the deposition. *It would have been nice,* I thought, *if Stuckey had called me. A call would have saved me the trip.* But he probably thought that I just loved to fly to LA and back for the hell of it. Right? But that certainly would not have been the fun thing to do. They would have been denied the laughter that undoubtedly ensued.

The election was a week away. I called Rod Blonien and gave him a rundown of Bradley's testimony. If they wanted to use any and all of it, it was fine by me; I had Ruth Barrett's OK. According to the polls, Bradley was still far ahead of Deukmejian. Blonien told me that despite the polls, they had their own polls, which indicated that Deukmejian would squeak out a victory, so they would not be using the information I had provided. Had they had a serious doubt about their own polls, they might have used my information. Although there had been publicity in the press and on TV about the Bland matter, it never really did become a major campaign issue.

Bradley thought it would be made an issue. On October 28 the *San Francisco Chronicle* reported that Bradley was publicly accusing Deukmejian of lying in their most recent debate and that Deukmejian had done a poor job of prosecuting Medi-Cal fraud cases as attorney general of the state. Quoting the *Chronicle*: "While Bradley was calling Deukmejian a liar, several of his aides were expressing concern that Deukmejian may try to close the gap in the polls in the next five days by launching 'attack' campaign television and radio commercials or a barrage of mailed pamphlets."

Assuming that the Bland matter was what Bradley had in mind as the subject of the anticipated attack, he never knew how close his concerns were to becoming reality.

26.

November 2, 1982—*Election Day.* As the voting booths were closing, and as election eve wore on, the predictions of a Bradley victory came into doubt. A large late surge of absentee ballots from conservative Orange County and Deukmejian's home area of Long Beach tipped the scale, and Deukmejian was the victor.

The win was by the narrowest of margins. Deukmejian had 3,881,014 votes, compared to Bradley's 3,787,669 votes. Deukmejian had 49.28 percent; Bradley, 48.09 percent.

The results as compared to the polling numbers led to a theory dubbed "The Bradley Effect." This theory, which is still talked about today and was especially pertinent in Barrack Obama's run for president of the United States, says that many voters, particularly white ones, might tell a pollster they are voting for the black candidate, but when they get into the voting booth, they actually vote for the candidate who is white.

The margin of victory was a mere 100,000 votes, and I wondered if the publicity that did evolve from our case was enough to tip the scales. I thought, perhaps egotistically, that this could be the case.

The story did hit many newspapers, major and minor, throughout the state, and there was TV coverage. I daydreamed that what had now become known as "The Bradley Effect" more probably was "The Barrett Effect."

27.

That evening I talked to Tom Prelock on the phone. Naturally, we were both ecstatic about the election results. We talked about getting together for a few drinks but decided against it, as we lived some fifty miles from each other, and neither of us wanted to face the prospect of a DUI. I did go down to a local watering hole and downed a few. But I came home early enough to take a walk with Max.

I have had many dogs in my life, and I have read many dog stories. But there has never been a dog like Max. Before my divorce, when I lived in the Bay Area, I owned a rental house in San Pablo. The house was quite run-down, and I had inherited the tenant when I bought the house on the cheap. The tenant was a weird old guy who didn't think he should have to pay rent to a new owner. After some haggling I served a three-day notice on him to pay up or move out. He decided to move out. In doing so, amazingly, he left everything that was in the house when he vacated. He left his furniture and furnishings, his food, everything. He apparently took nothing with him when he moved, except for his vehicle. Even the garage contained his tools, gas cans, workbenches, everything.

The backyard was surrounded by a chain-link fence. And inside the fence was a German shepherd. Fortunately, I was on the outside of the fence. The dog appeared to be extremely vicious; he first examined me with a low growl and then charged the fence, barking each time I moved. I went into the house through the front door and looked at this animal through the rear-door window. He moved to the rear of the backyard and watched me intently without moving a muscle.

He was a large dog but very skinny. I judged he had not eaten for some time, to the point where I would say the tenant could have been charged with animal cruelty. But despite the obvious mistreatment, or at the least, neglect, I could see he was regal. He was a proud dog.

The tenant had left a large sack of dry dog food in the kitchen. I filled a bowl and cautiously opened the rear door. The dog tensed and growled. I opened the door slowly, and making sure he was not about to charge me, I ventured farther outside to the porch and down the two stairs into the yard. The animal stared at me, tensed, ready to strike, but not moving a muscle. I placed the bowl of food down on the ground and retreated to the porch stairs, where I sat down.

I spoke quietly, enticing the dog to come forward to eat the food. Ever so slowly he approached. When he reached the bowl, he smelled the food. I had never in my life seen any person or any animal eat so much so fast. The animal was starving. He finished the bowl. I stood up, still talking quietly to him. He backed up into the yard. I took the bowl, went into the house, and filled it again. I returned to the backyard and put the bowl where I had put it before. The dog approached once again, this time more rapidly, and began to devour the entire contents of the bowl. Once again, I sat on the porch step.

When he had completed eating the entire second offering, he sat down and looked at me. I told him he was a good dog, a very good dog. He licked his chops and cocked his head.

"I'm going to call you Max," I told him. He seemed to like that, because his tail wagged, ever so slightly. "Max, you are a very good doggy, yes you are." His tail wagged somewhat more strongly. I extended my arms and he walked over, right into my arms, and I hugged him tightly.

His head went down, and then he looked up right into my eyes as if to say, "Thank you, John, I've been waiting for you for ever so long."

28.

The 1982 California gubernatorial election was over, and this was a good thing. What was not so good is that both of my Bland cases were not over.

In *Barrett v. Bradley*, Joseph Cotchett and Susan Illston hit me with a notice of motion and motion for summary judgment. In measuring this document with attachments, we should probably do so by weighing it rather than by counting the number of pages. By both measures, it was heavy and it was lengthy. All in all, I have always considered these motions to be a royal pain in the ass, regardless of which side I was on, whether I was making the motion for a client or defending against it. They are tedious and time-consuming.

Our case contained four causes of action. The motion would be heard as to all four individually. If the motion were granted as to a cause of action, that cause of action would be no more. These motions are brought with the goal of removing causes of action from the case so it would not be necessary to further deal with them. If the motion were to be granted as to all causes of action, the case would be over. That would be it; there would be no trial.

A motion for summary judgment alleges that there are no triable issues of material fact in a case. To support the motion, many documents need to be filed. Civil lawyers know what they are, and it is not necessary that a legal course be given here.

They attacked our first cause of action for breach of contract, admitting that, yes, there had been a contract between Bradley and Bland, but based on all the documents and evidence, Bradley had not breached the contract.

As to our second cause of action for fraud, their claim was that all the documents and evidence showed there had been no fraud on Bradley's part.

The motion went on to great lengths to show that Bradley did not breach any fiduciary duty to John Bland as was alleged in our third cause of action.

Regarding our fourth cause of action alleging a conspiracy between Tom and Ethel, their obvious contention was that we lacked any evidence to support this.

Finally, they argued that the statute of limitations had run out on all of our claims, because they had not been filed within the time period allowed by law.

They summed it up with a quotation from another leading case, "A summary judgment is proper to eliminate sham and baseless claims and pleadings." They were contending that our entire case was a sham and was baseless.

29.

I sat down to prepare Bland's legal pleading to oppose Bradley's motion for summary judgment. What I really wish I could have done at this point was to write the caption of the document, insert the word, "Bullshit," sign it, and have it filed with the court. But alas, the law books do not provide for such a response. Therefore, over a period of days, I prepared what eventually turned out to be twenty-two pages of factual and legal argument in opposition to their motion. The hearing at the San Mateo County Superior Court was eventually to be held on December 14, 1982.

Meanwhile, back in the Contra Costa County court, I had filed a motion to compel Louise Smith to give a deposition at my office in Brentwood. On November 17, 1982, after Felix Stuckey and I argued the matter, the motion was granted by Judge Martin E. Rothenberg. Smith's deposition was set for December 4. Rothenberg was a seasoned civil court judge who would often invite opposing attorneys into his chambers to discuss their cases. When things became heated, the judge would raise his arms as a signal for all to be quiet; he would then turn on classical music quite loudly and close his eyes. When he finally opened his eyes and turned off the music, the attorneys knew damned well to keep things toned down. He is also the judge who, in another case, denied my request to take judicial notice that an Austin Healy was a sports car. Lest there be any confusion, his decision on this issue was legally correct.

On November 19, 1982, I took the deposition of Ethel Bradley at Joe Cotchett's office. Susan Illston was there, along with only one court reporter this time. Ethel's security, as I recall, remained outside the room.

Ethel Bradley appeared to be a nice lady. She was somewhat on the quiet side, but friendly. Her answers to my questions concerning their dealings with John Bland produced very little. From her testimony, she was the dutiful housewife. Her husband took care of all their business dealings, and he did not tell her much about such things. Nor was she interested in any of the financial details.

Q: Did your husband tell you the bank would have to go up to look at the property?

A: My husband never tells me that, he just does what he wants to do.

Q: He's the boss?

A: He's the boss when it comes to that kind of thing.

She testified that Louise Smith, John Bland's sister, telephoned her all the time. Reportedly, Louise was upset that action was being taken against Tom and Ethel Bradley; Louise thought they should get the property and any proceeds from his estate because they had bailed Bland out in his time of need. Ethel further testified that Bland's brother, Emerson, repeatedly told her she was stupid for giving Bland $25,000.

Q: Did you know Louise Smith is contesting the will?

A: That is why she is doing it.

Q: To see that you get the money?

A: I guess. I don't know what she's doing it for.

And further:

Q: During each conversation she [Louise] has told you that she thinks you should have the property?

A: Yes, she said Johnny told her that, John Bland told her that, that the property was supposed to go—money was supposed to go to Tom and me.

Ethel denied ever hearing the name Felix Stuckey and said she did not know who had hired him to represent Louise. She then said a strange thing. When Ethel found out that Louise had a lawyer, Ethel refused to talk to her about the Bland situation and the pending cases. It was strange in that she previously talked to her all the time about these matters.

And finally:

Q: When you learned of John's death, did you feel you had any continuing obligation to make payments under that promissory note to anybody?

A: No.

30.

With the date for hearing of their motion for summary judgment coming up on December 14, I decided what was good for the goose was good for the gander, so I filed our own notice of motion and motion for summary judgment to be heard on the same date. Our contention was that there were no triable issues of fact with respect to Count One, that Bradley had indeed breached his contract with Bland. Defense attorney Susan Illston promptly filed papers in opposition to this motion.

31.

December 4 arrived, the date upon which Mr. Stuckey and his client, Louise Smith, had been ordered by the Contra Costa County court to be at my office for her deposition. As I fully expected, they did not appear. I then prepared and filed a notice of motion for order for sanctions, meaning we wanted the court to order some sort of punishment for their failure. The date of February 2, 1983, was set for Stuckey to appear to explain to the court why he and his client didn't appear.

32.

December 14, 1982, was a day of reckoning for the case of *Barrett v. Bradley*. This was the day upon which the motions for summary judgment would be heard. The judge who was assigned to hear the matter was Eugene McDonald. I had obtained a basic rundown on this judge from the deputy district attorney earlier, when he had provided information to me on all the judges in San Mateo County. I was not particularly a happy camper; while he reportedly was a good and able judge, he was said to be a member of the Democratic Party clique that prevailed in the county at the time. I could, if I were to decide, disqualify him, and I would not be required to give any reason at all. However, in any given case, you are only allowed to exercise this preemptory challenge one time. If I did that, I might be standing before one of the other judges who would be absolutely terrible for my case. And I might need my challenge later when the identity of the judge who would try the case became known.

The case was called.

Mr. Allen: John Allen appearing for Special Administratrix of the Estate of John Bland.

Ms. Illston: Susan Illston, representing the Defendants.

Judge McDonald: You left the heavyweight at home.

Ms. Illston: That's right, Judge.

The judge was obviously referring to Joe Cotchett, the heavy-weight. I was fighting these heavyweight attorneys who represented perhaps the most powerful Democrat in California, with the possible exception of Jerry Brown, the outgoing governor. And I was fighting on their home turf. I felt like the captain of my high school football team, and we were about to play the Green Bay Packers. Oh well, what are you going to do? Full speed ahead! Charge! It's all I could do.

In a hearing on a motion for summary judgment, the judge is to make the determination as to whether there is a triable issue of fact as to each cause of action. This hearing is not a trial. The sole issue to be decided is are there any facts that could lead the trier of fact—for example, a jury—to come to different conclusions. If the answer is yes, then summary judgment should not be granted. The judge should not decide the issues themselves. Are there facts to raise issues? If so, that's enough to defeat the motion.

We argued the matters for about an hour, and the judge proclaimed his decision on each cause of action. Ms. Illston was to prepare the order, and I was to approve it and submit it to Judge McDonald for his signature.

Later, Susan Illston and I could not agree on just exactly what Judge McDonald had said or how he had ruled. We both ordered the transcript of the proceeding. Even after reading the transcript, we could not agree on what the judge had said. We argued back and forth for over three months and could not reach an accord. Eventually, we had to refer the matter back to the judge to make the ruling.

On March 17 Judge McDonald rendered his order on the motions. The allegations of Counts Three and Four, those alleging breach of fiduciary duty and conspiracy, were thrown out. Count Two for fraud remained. Apparently, the judge did not believe that we had raised any triable issues regarding whether or not Bradley had breached a fiduciary duty to Bland, which should be heard by a jury. With regard to Count One, the ruling was made that I found to be inexplicable. As to this count, alleging breach of contract, the decision was that summary judgment was not granted in its entirety. The judge went on to make the decision himself as to the extent of Bradley's contractual obligation. He summarily decided this issue, even going so far as to calculate the sums that had been paid under the note and the sums remaining to be paid. He must have felt there was a triable issue of fact, in which case the motion for summary judgment on this count, in my opinion, should properly have been denied. However, rather than ruling as such, he had assumed the role of trial judge and made the ultimate decision himself.

As to Judge McDonald's throwing out our allegations of conspiracy, I thought he was correct, as I no longer believed Ethel Bradley to be responsible for any transgressions, based on what I had ascertained from taking her deposition.

But the end result was that our case had been substantially gutted.

Meanwhile, the press was reporting that Tom Bradley was already looking toward the 1986 governor's campaign. He also said he was considering running for mayor in two years for an unprecedented fourth term. He stated that he felt hurt by losing the election and what part he believes race may have played in the election.

"I don't think there would be any challenger on the horizon [in 1986] that I can think of that would be stronger than my candidacy," he said.

33.

Now that the motions for summary judgment ordeal was past, I could redirect my energy to the will contest in Contra Costa Court and that attorney on the other side, Felix Stuckey. I prepared and filed two documents. The first was a motion for sanctions for their non-appearance at the court-ordered deposition of Louise Smith.

The second was a notice of motion for summary judgment. I alleged that Stuckey filed the contest for the sole reason of delaying and obstructing our case against Bradley in the San Mateo case and that his filing was a pure sham. I attached Ruth Barrett's sworn declaration. These matters were scheduled to be heard on February 2, 1983.

In her declaration Ruth swore under penalty of perjury that she spoke with Louise Smith on the telephone on November 18. Louise told her she had not retained Felix Stuckey. She also told Ruth that she, Louise, had no interest in the estate and that it was never her desire to contest John Bland's holographic will. She further told Ruth that she did not intend to attend any proceedings, including depositions, conferences, nor the trial itself. She said she had made no payment to Stuckey. Ruth did not ask, but she felt that Louise had never even met Felix Stuckey.

On January 21, 1983, Stuckey filed a dismissal of Louise's contest with the court. He called me to tell me and asked that I drop my motions, which were scheduled to be heard on February 2. I replied, "No." Actually, I didn't use that exact word. More precisely, I used two words, and those were not professional in the least.

On February 2 we appeared before the Honorable Patricia Herron. The dismissal having been filed, the motion for summary judgment was dropped. The judge continued the issue as to whether sanctions should be ordered. They never were ordered.

The matter continued through the probate court, with Ruth Barrett now firmly established as administratrix and heir of the Bland estate. The matter was finalized in July 1983, the Honorable Norman Spellberg presiding. The total estate came out to less than $10,000, plus the remaining sums due from the Bradley Ltd. promissory note. Of that, I was awarded the magnificent sum of approximately $4,000 for ordinary and extraordinary services rendered. Plus, Ruth Barrett was ordered to pay me half of the net recovery from future payment on the note, which then totaled approximately $18,000.

The Contra Costa County will contest was over. At this point, the reader may have questions. One area of inquiry would certainly be why I did so much work, knowing that the monetary reward would be so small. Good question. I was into the case against Bradley, and the will contest was an offshoot. In order to maintain the Bradley case with Ruth Barrett as plaintiff, I had to fight the will contest lest her capacity as plaintiff be dissolved. The other side knew that. I knew that. Bummer that it was, I really had no choice.

Another question would be the reason or reasons I did not take action against Felix Stuckey, this pawn of an attorney employed to do nothing but screw me up and who used the courts to do so. I did start to prepare a lawsuit against him for abuse of process. I also seriously considered reporting his actions to the State Bar of California, which provides oversight over and has the power to punish errant attorneys. However, I did not follow through with either of these proposed courses of action; I simply let Stuckey drift off into the sunset.

34.

When I came home that evening and let Max outside, he returned and man, did he stink! He thought it would be cool to go out into the neighbor's pasture and roll around in cow dung. Why in hell he would do that, I had no clue. I did later look into the reason and discovered it has something to do with their connection to wolves. Wolves do the same thing. It is thought that wolves roll around in smelly things to disguise their scent to animals they are hunting.

Well, whatever the reason, although this may have been Max's choice of cologne, to me, and most humans I know, this is one downright nasty trait of animal behavior that I can do without. If this were the only trait of dog behavior, there would be no dogs. They would be wiped off the face of the earth.

It was cold that night, as are all nights in February on the Delta. I walked Max down to the river's edge and told him to jump in. He sat down and looked over at me.

But I don't want to.

"Jump in," I directed. He looked at the river and then back up at me.

But I don't want to.

"Max, dammit, jump in." I pointed to the water.

And so he jumped, swam around, exited the river, and came over to me, sitting exactly where he was before.

"Smells better, Max, but not good enough. Jump in!" He looked at me, looked back at the water, looked at me again, and jumped.

This repeated itself two more times until he was passable. I took him back inside, toweled him dry, gave him a treat, and we were down for the night.

And you know what? He never rolled in cow dung again!

35.

In April 1983 we did attempt to settle the Bradley case. We came close, but just could not quite get there.

Bradley's position remained that he had done absolutely nothing wrong. He further contended that Bland's estate had suffered no damages. He said he had previously agreed to pay one-half of the monthly payments to the estate as they came in; thus, another $18,400 would eventually be forthcoming to the estate.

Barrett's position was that more than that sum was due and owing. Our contention was that Bradley should not have reimbursed himself for the loan, which he took out with his bank, principal, and interest. He was into the "partnership" for absolutely no monetary outlay whatsoever. Bland was into the deal with his property, worth at least $55,000 at the time. Bradley had failed to place his agreement with Bland into the escrow, which meant that upon Bland's death, there would be no record of Bland's interest, and Bradley would receive all of the subsequent payments from Bradley Ltd. And in truth, this is exactly what happened. Bland died. When I first wrote to Bradley, he replied that he had no further obligation to Bland. In fact, he went further than that when he said he had no obligation to Bland in the first place. It was only when he was confronted with the evidence, in his own handwriting, that he confessed the truth. Now he was saying he always agreed there was the obligation to Bland and that payments would continue to be made.

We also contended that Bradley had overstated his expenses and owed the Bland estate the amounts that he had deducted from Bland's share.

We made what we thought to be a reasonable offer under the circumstances. We would accept the sum of $40,000 cash, with Bradley to retain all interest in the note.

Yes, we were close to a settlement, but no cigar.

Since there was no agreed-upon resolution, the case was set for jury trial on August 15, 1983.

36.

In April, May, and June, not having reached a settlement, I had no choice but to prepare for trial. Just what did we have that could give us a shot at winning? Our prime witness, who would have supplied just about all we would need and who would most certainly gain the sympathy of the jury, was John Bland, and he was dead. I was going to have to establish our case through Tom Bradley. This was to be a daunting task, because Bradley was slicker than oil on a wet pavement and as smooth as a fine whiskey from Tennessee. And as we already knew, opposing counsel was certainly the most formidable I had ever encountered or would encounter in the future.

I also felt we should have a real estate appraiser and a certified public accountant to testify as expert witnesses. The appraiser would tell the jury the history and development of the area and of the property itself and would provide evidence of fair market value during the years in question. The CPA would provide his opinion that, from his review of all the documents, Bradley did indeed defraud John Bland.

Expert witnesses are expensive, very much so. Neither Ruth Barrett nor I was even close to being in a position to afford one, much less two. Most fortunately, although I was not endowed with a great deal of money, I was always blessed by having great friends.

Dan Yee and Leroy Santos were among these friends, and it just so happened that Yee was a registered real estate appraiser from Richmond, California, and Santos was a CPA from Modesto. Both agreed to give it their all—and at very little cost to us. Although we knew our chances were slim, if we were to score big at trial, they would be rewarded accordingly.

I sent out a subpoena in an attempt to secure the records of the Riverside County Department of Public Social Services pertaining to Bradley's letter to them regarding Bland's effort to receive welfare payments. I received a letter from the chief of the inspections branch of that department, stating that he had taken the matter up with the county counsel of Riverside County. He was told he would be committing a misdemeanor if he produced these records, as they were confidential. So, dead end there. I might still be able to get this subject in front of the jury through Bradley himself.

The jury trial was set for August. There was the usual flurry of paperwork flying between the respective attorneys in anticipation of the upcoming trial date, including notices of depositions of the experts, notices to appear at trial, and a subpoena to Felix Stuckey to appear at trial with his telephone records, to which he objected by filing a motion to quash. We had disagreements all the way down the line regarding dates and locations of depositions and what requested information needed to be disclosed.

One huge problem, among all the other problems, was that although I had negotiated terrific financial arrangements with my experts, Yee and Santos, there developed a breakdown in communications. As a result, I now had no expert witnesses. The only witness I would be able to call to establish our case was none other than Tom Bradley himself. This was a bleak situation indeed.

37.

On August 10, 1983, another settlement conference was held at the San Mateo County Courthouse, this time in the chambers of Judge Melvin Cohn. The attorneys, with Bradley in attendance, spent the better part of the afternoon attempting to settle the case. Once again, the impasse could not be overcome. Trial was to commence the following Monday, August 13.

At this point I was asking myself why in hell I didn't call it a day, settle the case, and go home. My case had been substantially gutted at the hearing on the motion for summary judgment; I had no witnesses other than Ruth and Nolan Barrett, who were not around when the real estate deal transpired. They could testify that John Bland was a nice old man and that he left boxes of papers with them when he died. What else could they say at trial? Not much that would be admissible over the objections, which would certainly be imposed by Joe Cotchett.

The only way that I could possibly win this case, and the odds of this happening were exceedingly small, would be to call Tom Bradley to the stand and hope to trip him up so that at least nine members of the jury would believe that he did do wrong by John Bland. Could this happen? If I'm in a Texas Hold'em poker game, and I have a gutshot straight draw after the turn, will I hit my straight on the river with only four outs? Sure, it is possible. Not likely, but possible!

The downside of proceeding to trial was small. The worst we could do was to get the offer that Bradley had made—to send the one-half of the monthly payment received from Bradley Ltd.

So, OK, we had come this far. What the hell! We go!

38.

August 15, 1983. Date for jury trial. San Mateo County Courthouse. As I approached the courthouse front doors with my secretary, both of us laden with boxes of files, we and other entrants were delayed by uniformed officers as Tom Bradley, under heavy security, was scuttled inside. It reminded me of a presidential procession, with all the hoopla and finger pointing.

"Hey, do you know who that is?" a lady asked me.

"Nah," was my reply. "Must be somebody important."

"That's the mayor of Los Angeles! That's Tom Bradley! He just ran for governor!"

"You don't say," I responded.

We had been assigned to the court of Judge Lyle R. Edson. I did not know much about the man, other than reportedly he was fair, and—he was a Republican. I was not about to disqualify him as being the trial judge when I considered the possible alternatives if I were to do so.

Prior to the jury being brought into the courtroom, decisions had to be made on motions in limine, which were filed that morning by both Cotchett and me. These are areas that request that the other side not be able to bring certain matters before the jury. The end result of this hearing was not altogether unexpected. I was precluded from mentioning or bringing up hearsay statements of John Bland, his application for welfare benefits without first asking permission of the judge to do so, any prior lawsuits in which Bradley had been involved, and breach of contract issues; Cotchett was barred from addressing any contacts I may have had with the press or Governor Deukmejian's campaign.

Following this ruling there was not much left for me to present to a jury. But I was going to bring up the contract issues as they related to our case for fraud, as they were very much intertwined, and the fraud cause of action was all I had left.

The jury panel was brought into the courtroom. I was with Ruth Barrett at the table closest to the jury. Joe Cotchett was with Bradley at the other counsel table. Directly behind them was Sue Illston; other members from Cotchett's law firm were seated next to Illston. They were in and out during the course of the trial. The courtroom became electrified as everyone quickly realized that Tom Bradley, the celebrity, was in the courtroom.

Jury selection went rather quickly. After our *voir dire*, a teacher, accountant, two nurses, a Stanford grad student, truck driver, butcher, consultant, secretary, plumber, phone company employee, and a homemaker made up the jury. We also selected a real estate agent and a chemist as alternate jurors.

39.

The next court day, we presented our opening statements. As counsel for plaintiff, I went first. I explained to the jury that I expected to prove that John Bland was defrauded by Tom Bradley. In 1971 Bland, a destitute seventy-one-year-old man, told his relative by marriage, Bradley, about his property. Bradley viewed the property and liked it.

Bradley, an attorney, as well as being mayor of Los Angeles, agreed to be a partner of Bland. He would borrow $25,000 and bail Bland out from underneath his debts of around $20,000, give him $5,000, and take title to the property. Upon sale they would split the proceeds after Bradley recovered his expenses. I told the jury Bradley had not explained the fact that he would recover his entire investment, principal plus interest, before the split. I further told them Bradley failed to deposit their agreement into the escrow, and therefore there would be no evidence of any debt to Bland. This was particularly relevant, because Bland was older and in poor health. If he died, Bradley could keep the entire proceeds, and nobody would be the wiser. Further, the agreement was not notarized or recorded. The only document that was recorded was the deed showing outright ownership by Bradley and his wife, Ethel.

I also got in, without objection, that Bradley had done a will for Bland in which he, Bradley, was named executor and sole heir of everything Bland might possess at the time of his death.

At this point my notes called for me to tell the jury about Bradley's deceptive letter to the Department of Social Services regarding Bland's application for welfare. In light of the previous court ruling forbidding this, I skipped this portion of my notes in my address to the jury.

I continued. When Bradley Ltd. purchased the property, there was a down payment of $34,000. Tom Bradley used $23,487 to pay off his loan to his bank; $10,000 went to broker's commission. Bland received nothing other than a $5,000 advance to be deducted from his share at a later date. Bradley had received his money back, plus he was to receive half of the future proceeds from the note. What was additionally troubling was that had Bland himself listed the property with a broker, his recovery would have been substantially higher, at least double, probably more. I was telling the jury something I knew I would be unable to prove, because I no longer had Dan Yee, my appraiser, to testify as an expert.

I told the jury about Bradley overcharging Bland $76 per month against his share of the monthly payment and Bradley backing off when Bland complained.

I told them about my initial contact with Bradley before he knew what I knew about his transaction with Bland, how he had denied any obligation whatsoever, and how he subsequently contended he could not locate his records. I told them how Bradley, when he realized what we had, immediately changed his story by admitting the obligation.

At this point, my notes called for delving into the facts of Bradley's breach of contract, but I was precluded from doing so by the previous ruling of Judge McDonald. I was unable to talk to the jury about it.

So I hit hard on the only thing I had left, that Bradley had defrauded John Bland. I told them we would prove that Bradley had represented to Bland that their agreement would be placed into the escrow when Bradley bought the property, that it was not, and further that the proceeds of the sale would be equally divided, which they were not; that these representations were knowingly falsely made; that Bradley took more of the down payment than he should have; and that he had no intention of paying anything to Bland's heirs when Bland died. Had Bradley not lied to Bland, Bland would never have entered into the agreement.

I told the jury we would prove our case for fraud by a preponderance of the evidence and at the conclusion of the trial, I would be asking them to award reasonable sums for compensatory and punitive damages.

I thanked them and sat down.

40.

It was now Joe Cotchett's turn to address the jury with his opening statement on behalf of Tom Bradley.

Some of the highlights of his statement include: John Bland was constantly borrowing money. He was a flighty person who executed no fewer than five wills in the ten years preceding his death. He contended that our side would not be able to produce a single document to prove our case. He stated that Bland had been involved in numerous lawsuits before and that he never sued Bradley until I, Ruth's attorney, came along. He stated that recent monthly checks on the Bradley Ltd. loan had been made by Bradley and sent to my office, but questioned whether or not I had sent them on to Ruth or kept them.

He referred to Bland's many lady friends and problems he had encountered. He stated that Bland's last holographic will, naming Ruth as heir, was prepared within a month of him moving in with her, inferring that Ruth had placed undue influence placed on him. He stated that I had filed certain papers under penalty of perjury, inferring somehow that I had lied. He said he might call to the stand relatives of Bland, who would testify that they were abhorred by Barrett's lawsuit and lauded the Bradleys for helping Bland in his time of need.

"When I listen to Allen's facts, I'm in the wrong courtroom," he said. "I want you to challenge me."

All in all, despite my obvious distaste for most of it, I had to admit that Joseph Cotchett was truly one effective lawyer.

41.

The following day I called Tom Bradley to the stand. There he was, dressed immaculately in a suit and the perfect tie. He sat down in the witness chair and said, "Good morning" to the jury. It was as though he had invited them all as his guests. He was respectful and gracious, the same as he was to Tom Prelock and me, when I had taken his deposition at Los Angeles City Hall.

I knew I was in for a rough day. And my expectation was fully met. For seven hours I grilled him on the stand. Once in a great while, I felt as though I tripped him up, but not enough to establish our case or even anything the jury might find persuasive. Bradley was the smoothest witness I have ever encountered. You might ask him if it rained yesterday, and he would reply that yes, it did. Later you would come back, after it was established that it had not rained, and ask him the same question, "Did it rain yesterday?" "Oh, no, certainly not." But he never twitched a muscle or took a deep breath. There was absolutely no body language to indicate that either of his answers, although diametrically opposed, was untrue. And his demeanor was such that both answers appeared to be entirely true, although we know this to be impossible. Even when it was pointed out to him that he had given different answers to the same question, his manner projected believability. Maybe it was his smile, which seemed warm and genuine.

At the end of the day, I knew I was dead. I was dead tired, and my case was dead. Just done dead, all the way around. Even Ruth's testimony could not overcome the obvious upcoming loss. What could she testify to anything other than she knew Bland and could give a little history. And she could testify that he left some boxes of papers at her house. But the hearsay rule of the law keeps out most of his statements, other than those that might go to his state of mind.

I slept like a rock that night, and when the alarm went off to start a new day in court, I dreaded getting up. Breakfast was my final meal before the executioner was to pull the lever.

42.

The third day of trial, August 17, I was hit with paperwork the minute I hit the courtroom door. These lawyers who had been sitting with Susan Illston were not coming into and leaving the courtroom for the past two days without reason. When they left the courtroom, while the trial continued, they were back at their office diligently working to prepare paperwork to help destroy us in the trial.

Now, before the jury returned to the courtroom, I had to read and digest their newest entry, defendant's motion for non-suit. This was an eleven-page-plus-attachments document that asked the court to throw out our case. The law provides that, upon completion of a plaintiff's presentation of the evidence, his case may be "non-suited" if there is no evidence to substantially support a verdict in his favor. If granted, the case is over. It never gets to the jury. This is what they were now attempting even though this motion may have been premature.

I discussed the bleak situation with Ruth. Even if we were to survive the motion for non-suit, what were our chances of winning? "Slim to none" was the inevitable answer. We had fired our shot, and it had missed. Time to retreat with the least possible loss.

I discussed the matter with Joe Cotchett and surprisingly, their initial offer was still on the table—that is, future monthly payments received under the note would be divided between Bradley and Ruth Barrett. We immediately accepted, and the case was over.

Over. Done. Caput.

The reader may have been anticipating a more exciting storybook ending. The little guy pulls it out in the end and trounces the big guy, the crowds wildly cheering. Just like Paul Newman in *The Verdict*. But alas, though I wish it were true, the facts are what they are.

43.

The newspapers carried news of the case's dismissal the following day. The *San Francisco Examiner* reported my quote, "We had an especially tough time because our lead witness was dead." Reportedly, Joe Cotchett said the lawsuit never should have been brought in the first place, noting that the mayor had been trying to help Bland save property he was about to lose through foreclosure. Cotchett raised the possibility that the lawsuit may have been politically motivated because it was filed in the midst of Bradley's unsuccessful gubernatorial bid last year.

"Bradley, who said he was pleased at the dismissal, said he did not feel the litigation had any effect on the governor's race."

And so, the case of *Barrett v. Bradley* was over. What a feeling! I had originally hoped for a better outcome. But I was not all that disappointed. I was prepared for the eventual result and was relieved the ordeal was over. And Bradley was not governor of California. That was a good thing!

It was time to go home and feed Max. But, sorry, old boy, once you're fed, you're on your own for the evening.

44.

Some months after the trial, I received a call from Rod Blonien, who was now working for Governor Deukmejian. He suggested I submit my name for consideration as municipal court judge for the State of California. This was surprising because I never seriously considered the idea. Well, maybe occasionally in passing, but I certainly never discussed this possibility with anyone. After the Bradley case, my life had settled back to my preferred level of comfort, back to my country office with my shared secretary. My main concern now was whether or not to purchase a backup supply of IBM Selectric Typewriter balls as replacements for those that Carole was always breaking.

Rod and I talked for some time, and I eventually submitted my application and went through the interview process. The oral interview was in Sacramento with Marvin Baxter, who subsequently was appointed as justice to the California Supreme Court.

Time passed somewhat uneventfully. Then, on January 13, 1984, Carole excitingly burst into my office.

"The governor is on the phone."

"Yeah, sure, Carole," I replied.

"No, really! He's on the phone, and he wants to talk to you!"

"You're not kidding, are you?"

"No, he's on the phone!"

Governor Deukmejian was indeed on the line. I'm not sure as to the length of our conversation, but I would say it was at least ten minutes. He said my background had been fully investigated, and he would like me to accept the position of municipal court judge for Contra Costa County. I was humbled and flattered. I really did not expect the appointment. I accepted and within two weeks, I had referred all my cases to Don. I took the bench on January 31, 1984.

45.

Max was on the floor. Ah Christ, no! I had to help him up. I got him into the truck and rushed him to the vet. The finding was that his intestines were twisted and screwed up and that the situation could not be remedied. The only thing the vet could recommend was to put him to sleep. This was simply unbearable news. My friend, my buddy, who had been with me through thick and thin, who had listened to my problems, who never became upset or irritated with me, would have to go. I couldn't let the vet do what had to be done just yet.

I loaded him back into the cab of the truck and drove to the grocery store. There I bought two of the best steaks they had. We went home, and I dug a hole in the yard.

The hole being dug, I cooked the two pieces of meat, one for him, one for me. Although I knew he would not be able to digest his meal, I knew he would not have to suffer through his body's attempt to do so. We shared the meal. We talked and hugged. We reminisced about all that we had been through—the hardships, the problems, and yes, the good times, the laughter, the companionship, the love.

I went to the closet and took out the rifle.

"C'mon, boy, let's go outside." I led him over to the hole and had him sit right beside it.

"You have been such a good boy, Max. And such a good friend. And I am so very sorry."

I leveled the gun at him. At least I thought I might have leveled it at him. I couldn't be sure. My tears were running so fast that I couldn't see him. I wiped my eyes and tried again. I still couldn't see him. This simply was not going to work. I just couldn't shoot my best friend.

I led him back to the truck and drove him back to the vet. I waited for a while in the lobby as they took him to the back room. When it was over, they put his body in opaque plastic and placed him in the passenger seat of my truck.

The rest is fairly foggy to me, but I do know that I took him home, placed him in the open hole, and covered him with dirt. He was laid to rest between the new pine tree that I had just planted and the small oleander bushes.

Shortly thereafter I sold the property. But once in a while, I still return and can see from the road exactly where he is. The present owners have no idea he is there, but he's right there, right between that giant pine tree and those immense oleander bushes.

Epilogue

Bradley had been way ahead in the polls all the way up to election eve. But he lost by a hair, staging one of the biggest upsets in the state's history. In examining what had gone wrong with the polls, several ideas were advanced. The main reason that emerged became known as the Bradley Effect, which stands for the proposition that a white voter will tell a pollster he will be voting for a black candidate, when in fact he does not do so when he gets into the voting booth. The Bradley Effect has been considered more recently by the surprise losses of Barrack Obama to Hillary Clinton in the New Hampshire and California primaries leading to the presidential election in 2008.

Bradley decided early on that he was going to go after the governorship again in 1986. But his hopes were dashed as Deukmejian again was victorious, this time by a huge margin.

Bradley remained mayor of Los Angeles. In the late 1980s, he faced an investigation into his role in city funds being deposited into the bank of which he was a founder. In 1989 he was nearly forced into a runoff election by an unknown challenger. In 1993 he decided not to seek reelection to a sixth term as mayor. He died on September 29, 1998.

Today Tom Bradley is lauded and revered as one of our country's greatest African American leaders. Statues have been dedicated to his memory. Even that previously described terminal at the Los Angeles Airport has been named after him. To some he is a genuine American hero.

I rather enjoy fantasizing that the Bland lawsuit generated enough publicity to swing enough votes away from Bradley and into the Deukmejian camp to alter the results. It is quite egotistical of me to theorize that this could be the real reason, or at least one of the reasons, that Bradley lost the 1982 election. I realize this, but it sure is fun to think about.

To me, the ending thought to this is "whatever." Whatever was the cause of Bradley's loss, I can sure live with it. The world keeps turning and, as it does, I have absolutely no regrets.

Author Bio

John, formerly an attorney and now retired superior court judge for the State of California, works for the Administrative Office of the Courts as part-time judge in various counties within the state.

He lives in Northern California with his wife, Ryan, and enjoys traveling, boating, barbecuing, and playing poker.

John's website is johnmoreyallen.com.

www.ingramcontent.com/pod-product-compliance
Lightning Source LLC
Chambersburg PA
CBHW072024190526
45166CB00015B/391